After experience of teaching a........ ....ondary levels, John Harris worked for several years in Sheffield City Polytechnic where he was Co-ordinator of the Language Development Centre and, later, Head of Academic Development in the School of Education. He has also worked as Project Leader on a local part of the National Writing Project and as Regional Co-ordinator of the Language in the National Curriculum Project. He has recently taken up an appointment as Vice-Principal at the Institute of Language in Education in Hong Kong. He is co-author of *Reading Children's Writing* (Allen and Unwin, 1986) and of *In the Know – a Guide to English Language in the National Curriculum* (Stanley Thornes, 1990) and has written extensively on aspects of children's writing development.

Ronald Carter is Professor of Modern English Language in the Department of English Studies at the University of Nottingham. He is the author of many books on applied linguistics and was the National Co-ordinator for the LINC (Language in the National Curriculum) project from 1989 to 1992.

David Nunan is Associate Professor in Linguistics and Director of Research and Development at the National Centre for English Language Teaching and Research at Macquarie University, Sydney, Australia. He has worked as a TESOL teacher, teacher educator, curriculum designer, and materials writer and consultant in Britain and overseas and is the author of many books on applied linguistics and ELT.

Other Titles in the Series

Introducing
WRITING

John Harris

Series Editors:
Ronald Carter and David Nunan

PENGUIN
ENGLISH

PENGUIN ENGLISH

Published by the Penguin Group
Penguin Books Ltd, 27 Wrights Lane, London W8 5TZ, England
Penguin Books USA Inc., 375 Hudson Street, New York, New York 10014, USA
Penguin Books Australia Ltd, Ringwood, Victoria, Australia
Penguin Books Canada Ltd, 10 Alcorn Avenue, Toronto, Ontario, Canada M4V 3B2
Penguin Books (NZ) Ltd, 182–190 Wairau Road, Auckland 10, New Zealand

Penguin Books Ltd, Registered Offices: Harmondsworth, Middlesex, England

First published 1993
10 9 8 7 6 5 4 3 2 1

Typeset by Datix International Limited, Bungay, Suffolk
Set in Lasercomp Times Roman
Printed in England by Clays Ltd, St Ives plc

*This book is for Anne, Jeff and Madeleine
the best of friends and colleagues*

Acknowledgements

A great number of people have influenced this book, many without knowing it. Beyond a general acknowledgement to friends, colleagues, pupils and students, I wish to make a particular mention of my recent colleagues in the South Yorkshire and Humberside LINC consortium with whom several of the ideas in this book were developed – Jenny Cobley, Pat Seymour, Steve Anwyl, Roy Goddard and Jack Todhunter. I have also learned a lot from working over the last three years with the LINC regional co-ordinators but particularly with Ron Carter, the national co-ordinator. My biggest debt is acknowledged in the dedication.

LINC is the Language in the National Curriculum project that was established by the Department of Education and Science in England and Wales in 1989 to provide in-service training related to the implementation of the Kingman Report on the Teaching of the English Language. Copies of the Training Materials can be obtained from LINC Secretary, Dept. of English Studies, University of Nottingham, Nottingham NG7 2RD, UK.

The publishers make grateful acknowledgement to the following for permission to reproduce copyright material: *English in the National Curriculum*, DES, Her Majesty's Stationery Office, 1990; *Learning to Write* by G. Kress, Routledge & Keegan Paul, 1982; *The Development of Writing Abilities 11-18*, by J. Britten *et al*, Thomas Nelson and Sons Ltd, 1975; *Spoken and Written Language* by M. A. K. Halliday, by permission of Oxford University Press, 1989;

By permission of Basil Blackwell: *Literary Theory* by Terry Eagleton, 1983; *Language in the Inner City* by W. Labov, 1972.

For a full list of references, please see page 131.

The insights provided by work in applied linguistics can be of genuine support to all teachers facing the many complex demands of language learning and teaching. The Penguin English *Introducing Applied Linguistics* series aims to provide short, clear and accessible guides to key topics – helping teachers to keep abreast of this rapidly developing field by explaining recent research and its relevance to common problems and concerns. The books are designed for practical use: they focus on recognizable classroom contexts, suggest problem-solving approaches, and include activities and questions for further study.

Introducing Applied Linguistics presumes an increasing convergence of interest among all English language teachers, and it aims to be relevant both to teachers of English as a second or foreign language and to teachers of English as a mother tongue. As the relationship between linguistics and language teaching continues to develop, so the need grows for books which introduce the field. This series has been developed to meet that need.

The words that appear in **bold** type are explained
in the glossary.

Contents

Contents

Introduction

The teaching of writing is a vast and complex subject. In this book, which is designed to be an introduction to current thinking and practice, I shall, of necessity, be selective in the areas I cover.

In the first chapter I have chosen to concentrate on three topics. Firstly, I compare speech and writing since there are important points for teaching that follow from an understanding of the similarities and differences between the two modes. Then I look at the interrelationships between writing and learning which provide a significant perspective on much of what is contained in the rest of the book. Finally – since the book is addressed to teachers and teachers in training of both L1 and L2 pupils – I look at the typical differences between these two groups, noting that there are many similarities and that the groups are not in any way homogeneous.

The second chapter outlines some ways of determining text types, particularly in relation to classroom practice.

The third chapter considers how teachers can best help pupils to approach the task of writing – an area that is popularly referred to as **process writing**. I have consciously chosen not to use that term for the title of the chapter since 'process writing' has become associated with one particular and, as I shall argue, limiting approach to the teaching of writing.

The fourth chapter relates the ideas of the preceding chapters to classroom practice. In this chapter I address topics that are central to the teaching of writing – such as approaches in the early stages, what constitutes development, the relationship between reading and writing, and effective ways of teaching spelling and punctuation within the total context of writing.

In the fifth chapter there is a brief preamble in which I attempt to disentangle some of the issues over assessment as these impinge on writing. The main part of the chapter contains a number of authentic texts by pupils, together with extensive commentaries. This procedure will, I hope, serve to integrate the preceding chapters and give them also a touch of reality.

The books in this series are intended to be both introductory and interactive in ways that go beyond the usual province of written texts. At certain points activities are included, which either advance or reinforce the argument of the main text. I have not used activities consistently in each chapter, preferring to let them arise in natural contexts. In chapter 3, for instance, there is only exposition, while chapter 5 can be seen almost wholly as a series of activities.

I, as the writer, hope that you, as the reader, will respond to the activities *actively*. I hope also that you will respond to the rest of the book actively. I have been teaching, practising and reflecting on writing for over twenty years. This has made me certain of two things – that there are different emphases in the pedagogy of writing and that some will work for one teacher and some for another. It serves no general good to be polemic in the cause of one narrow and rigid set of practices. I am sure, though, that to be able to communicate a passion for writing and an understanding of the trials, the tribulations and, most important, the satisfactions it can give rise to is the surest way to help our pupils develop into successful writers.

1 Perspectives on writing

1.1 Speaking and writing compared

The following activity provides a starting point for exploring some
of the differences between speech and writing.

ACTIVITY

Read through the following transcript of part of a conversation
which is taken from O'Rourke (1990). If possible, work with a
partner and dramatize the dialogue by reading it aloud. The two
children are at infant school and are talking as they construct
something. Can you decide what it is? Make a note of particular
words and phrases that do not appear to convey adequate
information.

1a
Sarah: I'll draw a line . . .
Adam: I'll cut from the other side . . .
Sarah: What are you doing that for?
Adam: We've got to cut two triangles . . . then it'll be small enough,
won't it?
Sarah: Shall we leave that one like that?
Adam: No.
Sarah: 'Cos we only need two triangles . . . you . . . (indistinct)
Come here. So we only need two triangles?
Adam: Yes.
Sarah: Now what do we do?

Adam: Like that (gestures) *Now we've got to cut it ... Cut it there.*

Sarah: *Glue it.* (very quietly)

Adam: *Cut it.*

Sarah: (emphasized) *Glue it ... Why?*

Adam: *Because look, it's too big ... Cut it there.*

Sarah: *Which piece do we need?*

Adam: *That piece.*

Sarah: *So it goes just there?*

Adam: *Yes ...*

Sarah: *Does it curve or doesn't it curve?*

Adam: *No, it doesn't curve.*

Sarah: *But it makes a triangle piece?*

Adam: *Yes ...*

Sarah: *You stick one end and ... no ... and if we stick that just behind there ... No, it's just like a curve then.*

Adam: *It could be like that.* (gesture)

Sarah: *Yes, but we can't stick it when it's pointed.*

If you were able to discern that the two children are, in fact, making a boat you will have made either an inspired guess or an impressive piece of deduction. The words and phrases that convey less than adequate information include *it*, *that one*, *like that* and *there*. These occur more than once and as you read or performed the dialogue you are likely to have asked yourself: what is *it*? which *one*? like *what*? where's *there*? However, the two children understand each other perfectly well because they are sharing a purpose, an activity and a context. It would, in fact, be odd if they used full **lexical words** in place of these substitute words which are called, generically, **proforms**. For example, Sarah, instead of saying *Shall we leave that one like that?* would need to say something explicit such as *Shall we leave the piece of card which we have already cut to the shape of a triangle in its existing shape and size?* This sort of sentence would, of course, be so artificial in conversation that the partner might interpret the unusual and inappropriate form of utterance as indicating sarcasm.

However, if the children were to write an account of their construction activity, they would have to consider the needs of readers who were not part of the situation and they would therefore have to replace the proforms with **content words** (*boat*, *card*, etc.). They would also have to make the pointing expressions (technically called **deictics**) explicit. For example, *Cut it there* would need to be transformed into something like *Then cut the square piece of card across the diagonal to create two triangular pieces of equal size.*

There are three main ways of looking at the differences between speaking and writing.

1.1.1 Situation

Situation is an important factor for both speakers and writers. Some of the essential differences between speaking and writing in relation to situation are summarized in the table on page 4.

In stating what appear to be limitations on writers, I have passed over the possibility that writers can avail themselves of 'listeners' in the form of readers of a draft text. Readers of draft texts can, in fact, perform many of the functions of a good partner in a conversation, providing the reciprocity that is so supportive in conversation but which may well be absent when writing. This point has important implications for the teaching of writing and is explored further in chapters 3 and 4.

1.1.2 Grammatical choices

A second aspect of the difference between speech and writing lies in the typical grammatical choices that are made. Kress (1982) suggests that 'the main organising unit of the spoken text is not the

SPEAKERS

- can refer to people, objects and so on in the shared environment by pointing with gestures or by using 'pointing' words

- can check whether they are being understood by looking at the listener's expression, by asking or by being directly prompted

- in conversations (including telephone conversations) are encouraged by 'listener markers' such as *mm* and *yes* and – in live conversations – by gestures

- can backtrack and fill in information that may have been omitted – precise sequence is not a prerequisite of effective communication

WRITERS

- do not share an immediate environment with their readers and have to make explicit references to people and objects

- have no means of knowing once the text is finished whether the readers will understand the message – they need to anticipate potential misunderstandings and appropriate levels of shared knowledge

- have to find ways of motivating themselves to continue creating a text

- have to plan in order to achieve both a sequence and a selection that will lead to effective communication

sentence ... it consists of clauses of equal status or near equal status "chained" together in sequence.' He goes on to summarize the difference between the grammatical structure of speech and writing: 'Speech, typically, consists of chains of coordinated, weakly subordinated and adjoined clauses; writing, by contrast, is marked by full subordination and embedding.'

The conversation between Sarah and Adam working together (see text 1a) reveals an interesting corroboration of this insight.

The only obvious complex sentence (that is, a main clause + one or more subordinated clauses) is found in the last utterance by Sarah: . . . *we can't stick it when it's painted*. The rest of the conversation consists of either **simple sentences** (for example, *Cut it there*) or of clauses that sometimes imply **subordination**. Examples of the latter include: *'Cos we only need two triangles / Because, look, it's too big / . . . and if we stick that just behind there . . .* None of these clauses is developed into a fully explicit relationship with a main clause in a way that would be characteristic of written language. The last example is particularly interesting and shows the way in which speech has to be able to respond flexibly in order to mirror the development of thinking. Sarah starts to formulate a hypothesis *if we stick*. However, as she starts to say the first part, she has to revise her idea and so the completion of the original idea becomes unnecessary. This change of mind does not constitute an 'ungrammatical' structure; rather, it illustrates a major difference in the way that speech and writing operate. In writing, the hypothesis would need to have been thought through – that is, the writing would reflect a tested idea. Speech, on the other hand, reflects the process of testing the hypothesis and of altering it, if necessary.

Kress (1982) goes on to suggest that the syntactic unit we call a **sentence**, which is capable of great elaboration and complexity, is the fundamental basis of written text. An important aspect of children's development as writers is their ability to control and exploit the possibilities of the sentence. Kress further suggests that children's early writing often displays loosely **co-ordinated** structures – marked by clauses strung together by *and, then, so, but* – and appears also to be **chunked** (that is, divided into units) in ways that correspond more to coherent groupings of events or **propositions** than to syntactic units.

The relationships between sentences or utterances reveal another area of difference between speech and writing. Unless the spoken text is close to writing (as in a lecture or formal speech, which may in any case be read aloud from a written script or be based on detailed notes or cue cards), the connections in a spoken text are more likely to be revealed in the mutuality of the exchanges, in the sense that A asks a question and B answers and the answer is relevant to the question. For example, in text 1a Sarah asks *What are you doing that for?* and Adam replies *We've got to cut two triangles*. His answer is relevant to the question and the exchange has a unity that is formed by the mutuality of the speech.

In writing, the relationships between sentences operate at several levels. There needs to be thematic unity; there needs also to be a logical progression, often made clear by the use of **conjunctions** which express on the surface an underlying logic in the propositions of the text; there needs also to be grammatical linkage between sentences – called **cohesive ties** (see **cohesion**). In chapter 5 the analysis of 'Reflex actions' shows how these various relationships apply in a text.

1.1.3 Lexical density

Halliday (1989), in an important discussion of speech and writing, highlights further features that tend to differentiate speech from writing. Writing, he argues, displays a greater degree of **lexical density**. Vocabulary is generally divided into two major classes – **content words** and **structure words**. Structure words include items such as the articles, pronouns, conjunctions, modal and auxiliary verbs (*is, was, may, might, will, would* and so on), most prepositions and certain adverbs. This class of words is finite and 'closed' in the sense that it remains fixed and additions to it are rarely, if ever, made. Such words constitute a very small percentage of the total vocabulary of English but they occur with a very high degree of frequency. The other class, content words, is 'open', by which is meant that additions can be made – and they frequently are. Within a large body of language, even in specialized texts, the frequency of individual content words is much lower than that of structure words.

By lexical density, Halliday is referring to the proportion of structure words to content words in a text. He demonstrates that writing typically has a higher ratio of content to structure words than speech. This means that information is more densely packed into writing than into speech. This is demonstrated in the following activity which is presented without a commentary because it serves to reinforce the points just made.

ACTIVITY

Compare the lexical densities of the following two texts. One is the short transcript of Sarah and Adam that was used in the activity on page 1; the other is a short piece of writing by a 7-year-old pupil, used to provide a fair comparison. Count the number of content and structure words in each and work out the ratios. Your conclusion will illustrate the point about lexical density that has just been discussed.

1a (repeat)
Sarah: I'll draw a line . . .
Adam: I'll cut from the other side . . .
Sarah: What are you doing that for?
Adam: We've got to cut two triangles . . . then it'll be small enough, won't it?
Sarah: Shall we leave that one like that?
Adam: No.
Sarah: 'Cos we only need two triangles . . . you . . . (indistinct) Come here. So we only need two triangles?
Adam: Yes.
Sarah: Now what do we do?
Adam: Like that (gestures) Now we've got to cut it . . . Cut it there.
Sarah: Glue it. (very quietly)
Adam: Cut it.
Sarah: (emphasized) Glue it . . . Why?

7

Adam: Because look, it's too big . . . Cut it there.

Sarah: Which piece do we need?

Adam: That piece.

Sarah: So it goes just there?

Adam: Yes . . .

Sarah: Does it curve or doesn't it curve?

Adam: No, it doesn't curve.

Sarah: But it makes a triangle piece?

Adam: Yes . . .

Sarah: You stick one end and . . . no . . . and if we stick that just behind there . . . No, it's just like a curve then.

Adam: It could be like that. (gesture)

Sarah: Yes, but we can't stick it when it's pointed.

1b

Yesterday we went to Heaton park. We went on the coach. It seemed a long way. When we got there the driver had to find a place to park. When we found a place to park, we went into the park. We walk up to the animals. This is what we saw. We saw some peacocks. One of the peacocks was shoing off its feathers then we saw some hens then we saw some baby sheep we saw some horses then we went to the play area me and Julie went to the sea-saw then we went on the roundabout. Helen fell off the roundabout and cut her knee then we went back to the coach for our lunch. I had a bag of crisps.

(Author's data)

Two specific features that contribute to the greater lexical density of written texts are **expanded noun phrases** and **nominalizations**. The nature of an expanded noun phrase is best explained through examples. A noun phrase can occupy several slots in a sentence or clause but, for the sake of simplicity, I shall concentrate on their use in subject position. In each of the following examples the noun phrase in subject position is underlined:

(a) <u>She</u> mends cars.

(b) <u>The girl in the overalls</u> mends cars.

8

(c) *The cheerful girl who is wearing overalls mends cars.*

A noun phrase must include a headword; it can also have optional elements that modify the headword and occur either before or after it. In (a) the headword is *she* and there is no modification either before or after. In (b) the headword is *girl*. This is premodified by *The* and postmodified by *in the overalls*. In (c) the headword is again *girl*. It is premodified by *The cheerful* and postmodified by *who is wearing overalls*. Example (a) is a simple noun phrase; examples (b) and (c) are expanded noun phrases. Halliday (1989) suggests that phrases such as (b) and (c) tend to occur with greater frequency in written rather than spoken texts.

He also points out that nominalizations tend to occur with greater frequency in writing. The following examples of nominalizations are taken from one of the texts analysed in chapter 5 'The Wood Pigeon' – a piece of writing by a 10-year-old, Martin. Here we find: *Its normal flight . . . with quick wing beats*. In speech it would be more usual to find these notions expressed as: *It normally flies by beating its wings quickly*. The incidence of such features in written texts adds to the density and compactness of information.

It is important to stress that, in discussing these differences, I am in no way suggesting that one mode is intrinsically more complex or better than the other. Judgements like this have no part in linguistics. Both modes make different sorts of selections of grammatical structures to serve their purposes. What is important is to understand the differences and how these affect the writing and reading activities that pupils have to undertake in school.

However, we cannot ignore the fact that societies in general and education systems in particular both tend to regard writing as more prestigious than speech. Sometimes this view is even carried to the extent that the usages of the written language are regarded as the norm for all language use. Such an attitude reveals a profound ignorance and/or misunderstanding of how language operates. Linguistic research over the last twenty years has led to a clearer understanding of the different purposes for which speech and writing are used by society in general and by individuals; it has also promoted a better understanding of how these purposes are fulfilled. Unfortunately, popular and political understanding lags far behind. It is still common to find that people regard writing as the standard for language use and see speech as an inferior and corrupt form of the written mode.

This populist misconception also influences education, with the consequence that writing assumes an unduly dominant role in the assessment of learning and in the delivery of the curriculum. Even L2 learners often find themselves judged more by their ability to write in the target language rather than to speak it. Before looking in more detail at the situation of L2 writers I shall briefly consider the relationships between writing and learning.

1.2 Writing and learning

It is a common truth that much of our learning, in the most general sense, is acquired through language and that our perceptions of experience are, in turn, influenced by the inherent cultural bias of our mother tongue. Pupils, in fact, actively construct their view of the world – including value systems, beliefs and attitudes – through language. In the following comments I am taking this interrelationship between language and learning for granted and will offer comments only on the distinctive part that the process of creating written texts can play in the development of learning.

Writing is a process that occurs over a period of time, particularly if we take into account the sometimes extended periods of thinking that precede creating an initial draft. Even in the more immediately focused stage of constructing a text (actually writing the words down) writers pause, think, write, pause, think, revise and so on. This somewhat halting progress reveals the number of decisions that have to be made by the writer alone and also the extent to which reflection is an essential part of the process. These decisions and the reflection together both require and develop ways of thinking that are not the same as those developed through talking. Some of the decisions that have to be made in the course of writing are concerned with the interrelationships between ideas or propositions; some are concerned with revealing as precisely as possible the nature of certain experiences – giving them, in fact, a shape; others are to do with the selecting and ordering of ideas, information or experiences. All of these cognitive processes can and do occur in talk, but the way they occur in writing is fundamentally different.

1.2.1 Interrelationships

I have already described the way that clause and sentence relationships need to be made more explicit and more fully formulated in writing than in speech. It follows that the act of writing will increasingly require and develop an awareness of the range of possible connections between propositions, ideas and events. For example, children, in their early written narratives, will often simply juxtapose events with little evident sense of cause and effect. (See, for example, text 5b, page 102.) As control over the construction of narrative develops, it is likely that there will be a more conscious shaping in which the expression of cause and effect, and of action and consequence, becomes explicit. The act of making such relationships explicit in written language also enables the writer to reflect upon the truth of the stated relationships and to revise them if what is stated appears less than fully adequate. In the sense that language in general allows us to construct representations of experience, writing, in particular, allows us the further option of working on the representation. This is, of course, all the more true if, when writing, we are able to work through a process of assembling ideas, drafting and revising (see chapter 3 for a full description). It is almost as if the act of writing makes thoughts visible and tangible; this, in turn, provides the opportunity for revision and refinement because the thoughts are there on the page to be worked on.

1.2.2 Shaping experience

We have probably all had the experience of listening to someone who has just experienced something thrilling or traumatic trying to convey the nature of that experience – in a private conversation, on television or on radio. The result often verges on the banal as random images and memories are expressed without any real sense of the emotional impact being conveyed. This is not to criticize, rather it is to point out that speech (unless planned, rehearsed or scripted) cannot achieve the precision and significance that writing can, except in the case of a few gifted orators or conversationalists. The writer is able to reflect, and to order and experiment with words so that the experience is shaped into something of significance. This is obviously true of the great literary writers, but it is also true of pupils as they develop their ability to give significance to experience through this process of shaping in writing.

1.3 L1 and L2 writers compared

There are two major problems in attempting a comparison of L1 and L2 writers. The first is that there are many different groups of L2 writers; the second is that most of the research and case-study literature focus on tertiary-level students (see, for instance, Krashen 1984, McKay 1984 and Kroll 1990). And, indeed, much of the research suggests basically that the same factors are important for success with both L1 and L2 writers. These are the understanding of text types, the ability effectively to use the processes of text creation, and a motivation towards the act of writing itself.

At school level many L2 writers are children whose families have emigrated from non-English-speaking parts of the world to English-speaking countries (notably Australasia, North America and the UK). A distinction needs to be made between children who are already literate in their home language and those who are not. Children who are already skilful writers in one language are able to apply these skills to the second language, while children who are pre-literate or unskilled as writers need to learn the skills of writing at the same time as they learn the target language. A further distinction needs to be made between children who have to use the target language (English) as the medium of learning but who, for social purposes, continue to use their mother tongue and those who are learning English as a second or foreign language and who therefore use it for only a relatively small part of their time in school and none outside school. Finally, there are groups who are genuinely bilingual. Wales (1990) discusses some of these issues in much more detail from an Australian perspective.

Bearing in mind the enormous diversity of L2 writers, it would be foolish to make absolute prescriptions about how to teach L2 writing. Each group and, indeed, each pupil needs to be considered individually, just as L1 writers do. Information about and an analysis of individual needs are of paramount importance as a basis for developing appropriate strategies. Part of the analysis of needs will have to relate to the reasons why a group or an individual is learning to write in the second language. If, for instance, a pre-literate child has to learn a second language because it is the language of his or her adoptive country, the teacher has to be aware that there are few, if any, existing literacy skills or experiences to draw upon. Learning to write in English will also involve learning about the differences between speaking and writing and about the processes of writing itself. With pupils who are literate in their mother tongue, teachers need to be aware that there are existing literacy skills that can be harnessed to learning to write in the second language, provided that the learning about writing in the first language has set up habits and attitudes that are helpful.

Research into ESL/EFL writing has developed radically over recent years and now incorporates many of the debates concerning L1 writing. There is now much more emphasis on meaning than on formal correctness (see Brumfitt 1984, for instance). There is also an emphasis on process as an important part of the creating of meaning – with the product seen as the end point of the process and not as an end in itself.

These shifts in focus have implications for teaching and for assessment; they also have implications for teaching strategies and for the use of the L1, where appropriate, in L2 writing situations. One possible outcome, for instance, is that the teaching strategies will emphasize writing as a means of learning, rather than the learning of writing being the sole concern. In turn, this would lead to the argument that writing needs to be embedded in meaningful learning tasks and activities rather than set up as a discrete part of the curriculum. It would also suggest that the language features required for a particular learning task should be central to the language syllabus rather than a sequence decided without reference to need or to purpose.

There is another side to the issue, however. Traditions of writing, particularly in England, have fought shy of discussing important features of writing like structure and the details of language use. Notions of 'creativity' and 'self-expression' have become so dominant that the content is often the only aspect of writing that teachers are prepared to discuss, apart from the individual pupil who wrote the text. Happily, there seems to be a convergence of interests between the two traditions at the present time. And that should mean that the winners will be writing itself and our pupils!

SUMMARY

- Speech and writing are different ways of using language. Understanding the difference is an important part of the teaching of writing.
- Writing used in appropriate ways can help develop thinking and promote learning. It is up to teachers to ensure that the approach to writing in their classrooms facilitates both.
- Research indicates that the factors that govern success in second or foreign language writing are broadly similar to those governing writing in the mother tongue. Helping pupils understand the purposes and processes of writing should, therefore, be part of every teacher's aim.

2 Types of writing

2.1 Traditional classifications

Many attempts have been made to classify writing. The most long-established is the fourfold division of classical **rhetoric** – exposition, argument, description and narration. According to this system, pieces of writing are classified in relation to the writer's intentions: is he or she wishing to make a point, to report on something, to relate events and so on? This classical fourfold division has been a major factor in determining the writing curriculum in schools. The form that particular examples of writing take has also long been dominated by traditional forms such as essays, compositions and reports. Generations of pupils the world over have been required to demonstrate their intellectual abilities through the history essay, the English composition and the science report. Higher education has consolidated this tradition by giving primacy to the essay in examinations.

However, this tradition has had an unfortunate impact on the writing curriculum in schools over a long period of time since it has tended to give high esteem to types of writing that do not, in fact, have any real place in society at large. Thus, the essay and the composition, while highly valued in the world of education, play little or no part in the world outside. These forms flourished at a time when literacy was available to a small part of the population only and they still carry the hallmark of an elitist culture. The exception is the report, but that is a catch-all title that is applied to many, varied texts.

In recent years curriculum developers and Language in Education experts have expended a great deal of effort in reshaping the writing curriculum in an attempt to devise a more satisfactory and relevant way of looking at types of writing. There are three particular reasons for this which can be set alongside a general sense of dissatisfaction with traditional practices.

The first reason is that education is now regarded as the right of all pupils, not simply as the preserve of an elite minority. If you broaden the range of pupils participating in full-time education you need also to rethink the content of education. The writing curriculum cannot logically remain based on forms that are no longer practised; it must reflect and reinforce the types of learning that have accompanied the move to a populist education by emphasizing types of writing that have a wider currency.

Secondly, several studies have shown that development in writing is not a broad and uniform matter. The specific nature of the writing task affects development and, therefore, achievement. The most comprehensive attempts to describe development in writing have used relatively unsophisticated measures such as overall length of text, average sentence length and syntactic complexity (see, for example, La Brant 1933, Hunt 1965, Loban 1963 and 1976 and Harpin 1976). However, it has been shown that such measures are unreliable since each measure is dependent on the type of writing undertaken. What is needed is a much more sophisticated approach that allows for difference in text types such as narratives and reports, but, to date, no such approach has been applied to an extensive study of writing development.

Thirdly, assessment of achievement in writing is not a simple matter. Like development it, too, is linked to the type of task undertaken. At a time when several countries are developing national curricula or equivalents that are designed to assess the abilities of all pupils against sets of criteria (technically called criterion-referenced assessment), it is particularly important that the demands of different types of writing should be understood and that the specific types be described as accurately as possible.

2.2 Purpose, form and audience

One of the inherent problems with the many attempts to classify types of writing is that they look at one dimension only.

2.2.1 Purpose

Some consider the purpose of the text – that is, its communicative function. Texts can be grouped, for example, according to whether they are intended to entertain, inform, instruct, persuade, explain, argue a case, present arguments, and so on. However, it is obvious that the nature of the communicative function is not the only distinguishing feature of a text. Take the example of texts that are intended to persuade. At one extreme there are complex and lengthy reports about policy issues or such things as tenders for civil engineering projects. These are full of technical details but are intended to persuade people to a course of action. At the other extreme there are simple texts such as health warnings or posters supporting anti-litter campaigns that are also intended to persuade people to a course of action. From the point of view of the young writer (and, indeed, the teacher) there is a great deal of difference between the two types of text even though the same communicative function is present. Young writers could be expected, reasonably, to be able to create an anti-litter poster, for example, but not a technical report. Not only the technical know-how, but also the linguistic demands, would be clearly out of reach.

2.2.2 Form

This leads us to consider a second dimension, that of form. This term has become widely used in England and Wales since the introduction of the National Curriculum. It is broadly synonymous with 'text type'. By forms of writing I mean such things as: posters, brochures, pamphlets, letters, recipes, sets of instructions, lists, labels, stories, reports, poems, essays, playscripts, and so on.

If we were to consider form by itself we would face a similar difficulty to the one just described with purpose. Letters, for example, may have a common form. They will usually indicate the address of the sender and begin with a greeting. The greeting is usually formalized as *Dear Sir/Madam*, or it may be more personalized by the use of the addressee's name. It may even be a highly informal *Hi there!* Equally, we expect a letter to finish with a form of signing-off – conventionally *Yours sincerely*, but many other variations are possible ranging from the intimate to the abusive. The variation will depend on the purpose of the letter and on its intended recipient. The relationship between writer and recipient can be broadly characterized as ranging from formal to informal.

ACTIVITY

Consider the letters you have written recently and classify them according to purpose, noting also the readership for each. Then rank these letters in terms of their formality.

As you will have observed when doing this activity, there are many purposes that can be served by the letter form. The same is true of most other forms of writing. Thus we can gain a more precise idea of the nature of a writing task if we match purpose and form.

ACTIVITY

Consider the following table and decide which boxes represent impossible or unlikely combinations of purpose and form. The most striking thing about this activity is likely to be the number of combinations that you mark as possible. You are also likely to

PURPOSES FORMS	to entertain	to inform	to instruct	to persuade	to explain	to argue
Posters						
Brochures						
Pamphlets						
Letters						
Recipes						
Instructions						
Lists						
Labels						
Stories						
Reports						
Poems						
Essays						
Playscripts						

have marked some forms as having a range of possible purposes. Posters, for instance, can entertain at the same time as they inform and persuade. This shows that we must try to be flexible in the way we think about writing tasks. There is not always a simple one-to-one correspondence between form and purpose.

2.2.3 Audience

In discussing letters I suggested that the intended readership could be placed on a broad continuum from formal to informal. To explore this notion in more detail brings us to the third dimension in thinking about writing types – audience.

The concept of audience arose as an important consideration in the writing curriculum during the late 1960s and early 1970s. As was discussed earlier in the chapter, the writing curriculum had been dominated by traditional forms such as the essay. Writing by pupils was almost always addressed to the teacher seen either as an assessor or examiner – the person who told you whether it was a good or bad piece of work. In an attempt to provide more flexibility and a greater sense of reality in the writing curriculum, a greater diversity of audiences was proposed. The most comprehensive is the classification formulated by the writing research team at the Institute of Education at London University (Britton *et al.* 1975). This identifies the following categories of audience:

1. Self

Child or adolescent to self

2. Teacher

Child to trusted adult
Pupil to teacher, general (teacher–learner dialogue)
Pupil to teacher, particular relationship
Pupil to examiner

3. Wider audience (known)

Expert to known laymen [*sic*]
Child to peer group
Group member to working group (known audience which may include teacher)

4. Unknown audience

Writer to his [*sic*] readers (or his public)

5. Additional categories

Virtual named audience
No discernible audience

Although it was undoubtedly useful and liberating at the time as a reaction to the narrowly stultifying diet of writing in schools – Britton rightly points out how little writing at the time seemed to have any real sense of purpose – this classification does have some problems. A pupil may, for instance, write a journal and a formal literary essay for the same teacher. It will not be the audience so much as the nature of the task that determines the appropriate register of the writing.

A second consequence of such attempts has been to replace one artificiality with another. Whereas in traditional approaches pupils wrote only for the teacher usually perceived as an assessor, there developed a tendency to try to create 'real' audiences. Pupils were encouraged to write to local officials, to newspaper editors, to PR representatives of companies and so on. Often these so-called 'real' audiences turn out to be pseudo-audiences: pupils write to the assumed audience knowing that it is, in fact, still the teacher for whom they are writing.

It seems to me that it is much more helpful to the writer – and, therefore, more positive as a feature of the writing curriculum – to think about the nature of the readership for a piece of writing.

2.3 Readership

When writers set about a task what they need to know (in addition to the purpose and the form) is the nature of their readership. There are, obviously, many writing tasks for which there is a clear and unambiguous reader or readership. A personal letter is written to an individual known to the writer; an office memo is written to a known group of colleagues or an individual. Sometimes the reader is not known personally but by reason of his or her status – the head of a complaints department of a company, for example. Nevertheless, in the real world, there are many writing tasks for which a writer can have only a very generalized sense of the readership. What, for instance, do I know about the readership for this book? I know that the series editors will read it; I know that the publishing editor will also read it. All these prople have a professional and commercial interest in the text. What I do not know with any particularity is the wider, general readership. Nevertheless, I have to carry in my mind a target readership which can be characterized as people such as teachers and teachers in training with a professional interest in writing. It may also be read by researchers into writing but it is not primarily addressed to such a readership and this is indicated by the use of *Introducing* in the title. Such understanding of the nature of the readership influences the many decisions that have to be made in the course of writing. In large part the success of a writing venture will be to do with how well a writer gauges the readership.

It follows then that writers need to know as much as possible about a target audience to be able to communicate successfully. When they do not have sure knowledge they need to make educated guesses. Factors that need to be taken into account are:
— the formality or informality of the relationship between reader and writer
— the expertise of the readership – what degree of prior knowledge and understanding can be assumed?

— cultural assumptions – how far is it likely that the readers will share a common cultural background with each other and with the writer?

— attitudinal assumptions – are the readers likely to hold attitudes in common with the writer or has the writer to explain and justify his or her attitudes?

The writer's awareness of each of these factors will influence a whole range of decisions that have to be made when writing. Conversely, the failure of a piece of writing is sometimes the result of the writer making unjustifiable assumptions or misjudging the nature of the readership.

In terms of classroom practice, it seems to me more immediately realistic and helpful to build up pupils' awareness of such factors rather than to strive to create genuinely 'known' audiences or to postulate pseudo-audiences. There will, of course, be occasions when genuine audiences can be addressed. These should be sought after and utilized to the full. But it is pointless to pretend that all classroom writing can be geared to genuinely known audiences other than the teacher (see also Harris 1990).

So far in this chapter I have argued that for writing to be successful, writers need to know the purpose, the form and the readership for a piece of writing. I have also suggested that the notion of types of writing needs to be seen as a complex interrelationship of these dimensions. With this in mind we can now look at ways in which typical text structures and methods of organization have been described.

The following table shows how the dimensions of writing described so far are related to the rest of the section which deals with the ways in which texts are organized.

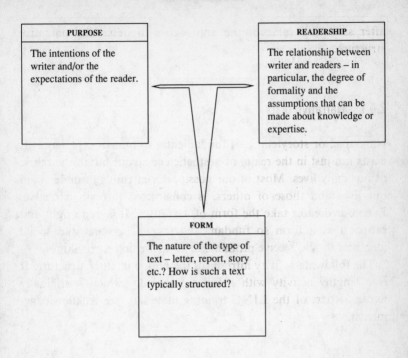

PURPOSE	READERSHIP
The intentions of the writer and/or the expectations of the reader.	The relationship between writer and readers – in particular, the degree of formality and the assumptions that can be made about knowledge or expertise.

FORM

The nature of the type of text – letter, report, story etc.? How is such a text typically structured?

2.4 How texts are organized

Describing the organization and structure of texts is a relatively new branch of linguistics. Even where persuasive descriptions are available it is not always the case that these can be related helpfully to classroom practice. Nevertheless, there is some work that is valuable and which is already being used in very positive ways in classrooms.

I propose to make a broad distinction between narrative and non-narrative texts or **genres** and will justify this distinction after surveying some of the approaches to describing narrative structure.

2.4.1 Narrative texts

Narrative, or storytelling, is fundamental to human experience. It exists not just in the realm of aesthetic endeavour but in the fabric of our daily lives. Most of our gossip, our attempts to understand our lives and those of others, is constructed through narrative. Even our dreams take the form of narratives. It is quite right and proper that a form so fundamental to our personal and social identities should receive prominence in the writing curriculum.

The following activity introduces the notion of story structure. It is a lengthy activity with a full commentary which I originally wrote as part of the LINC training materials (see Acknowledgements).

ACTIVITY

The traditional folk-tale that follows ('Lazy Jack') is, like many other examples of the genre, highly patterned – in the sense that there are repeated occurrences for each of the days of the week, with a significantly different outcome for each. This makes it particularly accessible for an analysis of structure. (At the same time, the story does contain portrayals and a moral ethos that we might want to question today. It is not, therefore, offered here as an example for classroom use, but as a means of describing how stories are structured in terms of their organization and purpose.) Read through the story. How would you divide the story into sections? What labels would you consider appropriate for each of these sections? (There is no need to worry about whether or not the labels sound 'technical'.)

2a

LAZY JACK

Once upon a time there was a boy whose name was Jack, and he lived with his mother on a common. They were very poor, and the old woman got her living by spinning, but Jack was so lazy that he would do nothing but bask in the sun in the hot weather, and sit by the corner of the hearth in the winter-time. So they called him Lazy Jack. His mother could not get him to do anything for her, and at last told him, one Monday, that if he did not begin to work for his porridge she would turn him out to get his living as he could.

This roused Jack, and he went out and hired himself for the next day to a neighbouring farmer for a penny; but as he was coming home, never having had any money before, he lost it in passing over a brook. 'You stupid boy,' said his mother, 'you should have put it in your pocket.' 'I'll do so another time,' replied Jack.

On Wednesday, Jack went out again and hired himself to a cow-keeper, who gave him a jar of milk for his day's work. Jack took the jar and put it into the large pocket of his jacket, spilling it all, long before he got home. 'Dear me!' said the old woman, 'you should have carried it on your head.' 'I'll do so another time,' said Jack.

So on Thursday, Jack hired himself again to a farmer, who agreed to give him a cream cheese for his services. In the evening Jack took the cheese, and went home with it on his head. By the time he got home the cheese was all spoilt, part of it being lost, and part matted with his hair. 'You stupid lout,' said his mother, 'you should have carried it very carefully in your hands.' 'I'll do so another time,' replied Jack.

On Friday, Lazy Jack again went out, and hired himself to a baker, who would give him nothing for his work but a large tomcat. Jack took the cat, and began carrying it very carefully in his hands, but in a short time pussy scratched him so much that he was compelled to let it go.

When he got home, his mother said to him, 'You silly fellow, you should have tied it with string, and dragged it along after you.' 'I'll do so another time,' said Jack.

So on Saturday, Jack hired himself to a butcher, who rewarded him by the handsome present of a shoulder of mutton. Jack took the mutton, tied it to a string, and trailed it along after him in the dirt, so that by the time he had got it home the meat was completely spoilt. His mother was this time quite out of patience with him, for the next day was Sunday, and she was obliged to do with cabbage for her dinner. 'You ninney-hammer,' she said to her son; 'you should have carried it on your shoulder.' 'I'll do so another time,' replied Jack.

On the next Monday, Lazy Jack went once more and hired himself to a cattle-keeper, who gave him a donkey for his trouble. Jack found it hard to hoist the donkey on his shoulders, but at last he did it, and began walking slowly home with his prize. Now it happened that in the course of his journey there lived a rich man with his only daughter, a beautiful girl, but deaf and dumb. Now she had never laughed in her life, and the doctors said she would never speak till somebody made her laugh. This young lady happened to be looking out of the window when Jack was passing with the donkey on his shoulders, with the legs sticking up in the air, and the sight was so comical and strange that she burst out into a great fit of laughter, and immediately recovered her speech and hearing. Her father was overjoyed, and fulfilled his promise by marrying her to Lazy Jack, who was thus made a rich gentleman. They lived in a large house, and Jack's mother lived with them in great happiness until she died.

Here is one attempt to divide the story into sections; the sections labelled A, B, C etc. are glossed later in the commentary.

/ Once upon a time there was a boy whose name was Jack, and he lived with his mother on a common. They were very poor, and the

A *old woman got her living by spinning, but Jack was so lazy that he would do nothing but bask in the sun in the hot weather, and sit by the corner of the hearth in the winter-time. So they called him Lazy Jack. His mother could not get him to do anything for her, / and at*

B *last told him, one Monday, that if he did not begin to work for his porridge she would turn him out to get his living as he could. /*

C / This roused Jack, and he went out and hired himself for the next day to a neighbouring farmer for a penny; but as he was coming home, never having had any money before, he lost it in passing over a brook. 'You stupid boy,' said his mother, 'you should have put it in your pocket.' 'I'll do so another time,' replied Jack. /

D / On Wednesday, Jack went out again and hired himself to a cow-keeper, who gave him a jar of milk for his day's work. Jack took the jar and put it into the large pocket of his jacket, spilling it all, long before he got home. 'Dear me!' said the old woman, 'you should have carried it on your head.' 'I'll do so another time,' said Jack. /

E / So on Thursday, Jack hired himself again to a farmer, who agreed to give him a cream cheese for his services. In the evening Jack took the cheese, and went home with it on his head. By the time he got home the cheese was all spoilt, part of it being lost, and part matted with his hair. 'You stupid lout,' said his mother, 'you should have carried it very carefully in your hands.' 'I'll do so another time,' replied Jack. /

F / On Friday, Lazy Jack again went out, and hired himself to a baker, who would give him nothing for his work but a large tomcat. Jack took the cat, and began carrying it very carefully in his hands, but in a short time pussy scratched him so much that he was compelled to let it go. When he got home, his mother said to him, 'You silly fellow, you should have tied it with string, and dragged it along after you.' 'I'll do so another time,' said Jack. /

G / So on Saturday, Jack hired himself to a butcher, who rewarded him by the handsome present of a shoulder of mutton. Jack took the mutton, tied it to a string, and trailed it along after him in the dirt, so that by the time he had got it home the meat was completely spoilt. His mother was this time quite out of patience with him, for the next day was Sunday, and she was obliged to do with cabbage for her dinner. 'You ninney-hammer,' she said to her son; 'you should have carried it on your shoulder.' 'I'll do so another time,' replied Jack. /

29

/*On the next Monday, Lazy Jack went once more and hired*

H *himself to a cattle-keeper, who gave him a donkey for his trouble. Jack found it hard to hoist the donkey on his shoulders, but at last he did it, and began walking slowly home with his prize.* / *Now it happened that in the course of his journey there lived a rich man with his only daughter, a beautiful girl, but deaf and dumb. Now she had never laughed in her life, and the doctors*

I *said she would never speak till somebody made her laugh. This young lady happened to be looking out of the window when Jack was passing with the donkey on his shoulders, with the legs sticking up in the air, and the sight was so comical and strange that she burst out into a great fit of laughter, and immediately recovered her speech and hearing.* / *Her father was overjoyed, and fulfilled his promise by marrying her to Lazy Jack, who was thus*

J *made a rich gentleman. They lived in a large house, and Jack's mother lived with them in great happiness until she died.* /

Dividing the story into sections

Although it will be argued later that the traditional terms – beginning, middle and end – are not satisfactory for analysing stories, these will be used initially to identify the major sections.

THE MIDDLE

The first thing to establish is how to subdivide the text. It is easy enough to identify the episodes that have a repeated pattern, and these are labelled C, D, E, F, G and H. Each of these episodes could be further subdivided, since each consists of an action (Jack hires himself for a day's work) and a result. The result, we should note, consists of three parts:

— he receives a reward for his day's work
— he mishandles the reward by applying yesterday's lesson to today's reward – except in episode C
— his mother scolds him.

Each of these episodes, therefore, concludes unhappily, since neither Jack nor his mother can resolve the problem of Jack successfully *working for his porridge*. Overall, we can see that this sequence of episodes represents Jack's attempts to prevent his mother carrying out her threat to throw him out of the house.

THE BEGINNING

Both the initial and the end part of the story provide more complicated problems. The first paragraph, for instance, can be regarded as the beginning, but we need to investigate a bit further and see what this means.

At the very beginning we find a phrase *Once upon a time* that is commonly called a 'story-marker' for obvious reasons. The next three sentences provide us with details about the life lived by Jack and his mother and the particular problems of Jack's laziness. The actions described by the verbs in this section are not one-off but habitual, answering the question 'What used to happen?'

In the fourth sentence, however, there is a change. The first verb phrase is still indicating past habitual time (*could not get*), but the next is not: *told* is a one-off action occurring specifically one Monday. This change provides the reason for the division made between A and B. A sets the scene and tells us about the circumstances that provide the background to the sequence of events we have already considered. B, however, sets the story in motion, and is the first of a series of events set in specific time (*on Wednesday, on Thursday, on Friday, on Saturday, on the next Monday*).

THE END

The two sections of the story that we have labelled I and J clearly bring about a conclusion. But this is achieved in a rather roundabout manner. Episode H differs from the preceding episodes (C–G) in that the result has only two of its usual three parts. The sequence is interrupted by a sub-plot, or **embedded** narrative, that concerns the rich man and his daughter. This embedded narrative could be analysed into constituent elements, but for present purposes we can simply note that the resolution of the embedded narrative also provides the resolution of the main narrative. The resolution of the embedded narrative occurs in I (*she burst into a great fit of laughter and immediately recovered her speech and hearing*), while the overall resolution of Jack's story occurs in J (*who was thus made a rich gentleman*).

As has been indicated, there are varying levels of detail that can be included in an analysis of the story. The degree of detail will, by and large, depend on the purposes of analysis.

So far we have accepted the over-simple terms 'beginning', 'middle' and 'end', but these terms, as we have suggested earlier, do not help us to identify the constituent elements or the functions within the total narrative of these sections. A way of labelling the elements and describing their functions is presented opposite.

This attempt to analyse the elements in a story actually advances us well beyond beginnings, middles and ends. We can now see that structures may well be more complex and that labels that give some indication of the constituent elements and their function are more useful. This is particularly significant in narratives that do not inevitably follow a simple time sequence. It is possible, for instance, to find stories that begin with the initiating action or even a subsequent episode or event and then backtrack to establish the scene-setting elements. In considering such stories the simple notion of beginning, middle and end would not help at all. It would, in fact, be highly misleading.

Other perspectives on narrative

There have been many attempts to describe the structures of stories. Often these have been made in pursuit of another goal (Labov, for instance, developed his well-known analysis when he was investigating the styles of oral storytelling he found common in the Black culture of Harlem). This does not invalidate the

LABELLING THE ELEMENTS

Section	Constituents	Function
A	situation and main characters and their circumstances	to set the scene
B	action that precipitates the ensuing events of the narrative	to start the story in motion
C–H	episodes that contain events describing the attempts to resolve the situation established in A and B	to advance the story
I	embedded narrative and resolution of this through the stupidity of Jack carrying his donkey	to bring the story to a climax
J	resolution of initial problem (Jack becomes rich) and statement of fairy-tale ending	to indicate the successful conclusion of the story

You could label the sections as follows:

A	scene setting
B	initiating action or event
C–H	sequence of episodes or events
I	sub-plot or embedded narrative
J	resolution or outcome.

descriptions: it can, indeed, make them particularly useful to apply to the stories written by young children. However, it does mean that the descriptions may need to be developed further to enable us to handle sophisticated narratives.

One of the simplest models is the Problem–Solution pattern which has been identified by Hoey (1983) among others. He identifies the basic pattern as follows:

PROBLEM–SOLUTION PATTERN

Situation	What was the situation?
Problem	What was the problem?
Solution	What was the solution/response?
Evaluation	How successful was it?

The evaluation can be either negative or positive. If negative, then another attempt at a solution may be made. This pattern is, of course, capable of considerable complication when negative evaluations multiply.

Labov (1972), as already noted, derived his model from oral narratives. He identifies six elements, as follows:

LABOV'S NARRATIVE STRUCTURE

Abstract	What, in a nutshell, is the story about?
Orientation	What, who, where, when?
Complicating action	Then what happened?
Evaluation	So what? Why is this interesting? What is the point of the story?
Resolution	What finally happened?
Coda	That's it, I've finished and am bridging back to the present situation.

It is perhaps relevant to point out straight away that the elements of Labov's model that are most particular to oral storytelling are the abstract and the coda. These elements frame the narrative, setting it apart from the surrounding social discourses. Obviously they are not usually necessary in written narratives. However, elements do remain such as titles (which can be seen as an abstract) and fairy-tale endings (which can be seen as a coda – for example, *They all lived happily ever after* or *It was all a dream*).

In work developed in Australia by Martin and Rothery (1980), Labov's model was used to differentiate between the simplest of emergent written genres – the observation/comment and narrative. They use three elements only: Orientation, Complication, Resolution.

A more sophisticated model was developed by Longacre (1976), who identifies the following elements:

LONGACRE'S NARRATIVE STRUCTURE

Aperture	the *Once upon a time* type of opening
Exposition	containing vital information about time, place, 'local colour' and participants
Inciting moment	the moment when things start moving in a story, when the predictable movement of the exposition is broken into
Developing conflict	when the action intensifies
Climax	when matters come to a head and confrontation and final show-down become inevitable
Denouement	a crucial final event occurs and makes resolution possible
Final suspense	details of the resolution are finally worked out
Conclusion	some sort of satisfactory end is arrived at

(A further category of 'peak' indicates the main point of the story and is analogous to evaluation in Labov's model.)

These models can be presented alongside each other as follows:

MODELS OF NARRATIVE STRUCTURE

Hoey	Labov	Martin & Rothery	Longacre
	Abstract		Aperture
Situation	Orientation	Orientation	Exposition
Problem	Complicating action	Complication	Inciting moment
	Evaluation		Developing conflict
			Climax
Solution	Resolution	Resolution	Denouement
Evaluation	Coda		Final suspense
			Conclusion

The analysis so far is suited to short and simple narratives. This is likely to make it useful for working with young and/or inexperienced writers. Planning strategies based on these analyses are presented in the next chapter.

There are descriptions of narrative that are much more ambitious and help us to understand more about how complex narratives can be organized, but they do not offer the same sort of structural guidelines that I have so far been considering. Particularly helpful is the work of Genette (see Eagleton 1983 and Toolan 1988). He suggests that the following categories are significant.

ORDER

The time order of the text. This may be organized to anticipate events, use flashback or play with discordances between the order in which events occur in the structure of the text and the order in which those events would have occurred in 'actual' time.

DURATION

A narrative can cut out, expand or sum up events.

FREQUENCY

An event in a narrative can happen:
— once and be narrated once
— once and be narrated several times
— several times and be narrated only once.

MOOD

This category has two subdivisions:
— Distance – the relationship between the narrative itself and the events on which it is based: these may be recounted or represented, told in direct or indirect speech
— Perspective
The narrator may:
— know more than the characters
— know less than them
— know as much and no more
The narrative, therefore, may be related by:
— an all-knowing narrator from outside the action
— one character from inside the narrative and from an unchanging viewpoint
— one character but from changing viewpoints
— several characters from a variety of viewpoints.

VOICE

This deals with the act of narrating: the narrator may tell events before, after or as they occur; he or she may be absent or in the narrative, may be a main actor or may play only a supporting role in the events.

2.4.2 Non-narrative texts

As I have already suggested, within the realm of non-narrative writing there are many problems of definition. To begin to provide some sort of a map of the area, consider the following activity.

Here are three opening sentences. Read them and then develop three texts by providing six or eight sentences that could follow from each starting sentence to create a coherent text.

2b

1. *Once upon a time there lived a small green frog called Freda.*
2. *First wash and fillet the fish.*
3. *Aggression between nations is caused by many factors.*

Sentence 1 is familiar ground – a story-starter clearly marked by *Once upon a time* and *there lived.* Your own text is likely to have developed the setting, set up a problem or complicating action and then, after some consequent actions or events, reached a conclusion. The events will have followed a broadly established chronology – not of actual, but imagined, time.

Sentence 2 will also have prompted a time sequence. In this case it will have been a projection of activities in actual time. The activities described are likely to be answers to a question such as, 'After washing and filleting the fish, what do you do next?' The answer is likely to be something along the lines of *Dust with seasoned flour and fry gently in clarified butter.* Further actions will follow and the conclusion will be the last action to complete the making of a successful dish. It may be, however, that a second series of actions needs to be described – for preparing a sauce, for instance – which has to be done at the same time as the cooking of the fish. This is typical of recipes and can create great frustration if the whole activity has not been thought through. This backtracking in time is

usually marked by *Meanwhile*... Nevertheless, in general terms
sentence 2 will have prompted texts that follow a time sequence.

Sentence 3 is not so straightforward. From this starter various
possibilities open up.

3(a) The sentence could be a general statement that leads to an
account of a specific incident, as in:

*Aggression between nations is caused by many factors. In the war
between Great Britain and Argentina, it was the occupation of the
Falkland Islands that sparked off the conflict. The dispute over
ownership goes back a long way in time, but the actual fighting
started after the occupation. The first event in the war was the
despatch of a British task-force to the South Atlantic . . .*

The pattern is then established for an account which is broadly
chronological but in which there may be passages of comment
outside the time sequence.

3(b) The sentence could be a general comment that leads to a
listing of factors, as in:

*Aggression between nations is caused by many factors. Fear, envy or
the personal ambitions of a head of state are among the most
common. We also find wars occurring because of boundary disputes,
language differences and trading rivalry . . .*

3(c) It is also possible that the opening sentence is set up as a point
of contrast with what is to follow. This, of course, is much less easy
to predict from just the opening sentence. An example might be:

*Aggression between nations is caused by many factors. Fear, envy
and the personal ambitions of a head of state are among the most
common. In civil wars, however, we usually find different factors
operating. Religious, tribal or political differences frequently provoke
internal strife.*

In 3(a) the text follows a time sequence, but in 3(b) and 3(c) there
is no time factor involved.

TIME

This activity points to one of the major organizational distinctions within the category of non-narrative texts. Some texts will be organized in accord with a time sequence; others will not. This distinction is described as **chronological** and **non-chronological** by some authorities (see Perera 1984 and DES 1990). I prefer to use the terms 'time-related' and 'non-time-related' (Harris and Wilkinson 1986). To clarify how this distinction relates to narrative and non-narrative the following table is useful.

TIME-RELATED OR CHRONOLOGICAL TEXTS		NON-TIME-RELATED OR NON-CHRONOLOGICAL TEXTS
Narrative	**Non-narrative**	**All non-narrative**
stories	lists	lists and classifications
narrative poems	recipes	(e.g. groupings)
such as ballads	instructions	arguments
autobiography	reports of –	comparisons
	activities	speculations
	experiments	descriptions of features,
	events	places, mechanisms
	processes	personal reflections
	(and so on)	(and so on)
Note. Stories and ballads can be either fiction or non-fiction or even a mixture of the two.		

The category of non-narrative, time-related texts includes some types that have relatively fixed configurations. Recipes, for instance, commonly begin with a list of ingredients, then continue with a step-by-step description of procedures to be followed. They are also characterized by the use of imperatives and by the deletion of certain items such as the determiner in *Liquidize mixture*.

Instructions are more complex and varied, though in simple

form a set of instructions may have a similar structure to a recipe. Instructions on how to play a simple board game, for example, are likely to begin with a statement of the number of players and of the age range for which it is appropriate. This is usually followed by a statement of the aim and a description of a set of procedures for playing. However, with many games the procedures are constrained by rules. If the rules are complex and the procedures unpredictable, the instructions are unlikely to follow a sequence of activities. In these cases the instructions will not be time sequenced, but will rather consist of a list of rules in which the ordering is determined by priorities or by the likely occurrence of situations. This should alert us to a general proviso – that the categories of time-related and non-time-related can never safely be regarded as absolute. Many texts will combine both types of organization, possibly at different locations in the one text.

Another issue that can be raised in this context is that while there is a generic likeness between the simple instructions for a board game such as Snakes and Ladders and a computer manual, in the actual detail of the texts this likeness will not be obvious. Both have a common purpose – to instruct – but the form and the readership are radically different and the resulting texts are very different too.

The report is also a highly varied category. At one extreme a report can be a recount of an event, as in the following example.

ACTIVITY

Read the following report of an event and work out the elements that make up its structure. Use your own labels to describe these elements.

2c

Yesterday was the Dragon Boat Festival. I went with some friends to watch the races. There were flags all along the road to the beach.

*The boats had flags on them and were painted to look like dragon
scales on the sides. There were several races but I don't know who
won. Then we had some hot dogs. It was a good day and I enjoyed
my holiday.*
(Author's data)

This simple report or recount has the following structure:
— Setting or Orientation
— Events with/without comment
— Concluding comment or evaluation
The linguistic features are similar to those of a narrative – the use
of the simple past tense, time adverbials and a consistent person (in
this example it is the first person *I*).

However, as I suggested earlier, another favoured type of school
writing is the science report. At its simplest this may be organized
like a recount in that it reports on a series of observations, as in
this example taken from Hoey (1986).

2d

HOT SOUP EXPERIMENT   LARA

Equipment
Bunsen Burner   *Soup Powder*
Tripod   *Mixing Rod*
Asbestos Mat   *Water*
Wire Gauze   *Thermometer*
Glass Beaker

Experiment
To see if soup is hotter in a container with a lid on or off.

What we did
*First of all we set up our equipment as in the diagram i.e. Asbestos
mat on the table, tripod on the mat, metal grid on the tripod, beaker*

*on the grid. Water in the beaker. Underneath the tripod is a bunsen
burner which is attached to a gas tap.*
*We lit the bunsen burner and took the temperature. It was 39°
centigrade. Then we waited for it to boil. When it had boiled we
again took the temperature. This time it was 100° centigrade. Then
we poured the soup powder into the water and using the mixing rod
we stirred it until all the lumps had gone. Then we poured it into two
containers putting a lid on one and leaving the other one open. We
waited for fifteen minutes.*

Result
*The soup in the container with a lid was hotter than the other one. It
was 70° centigrade whilst the other one was 63½° centigrade.*

Although there is a basic sequence of events, the structure of the
science report calls for additional items – the list of equipment, the
statement of purpose and the result. Each part of the structure has
a different linguistic configuration. The events or procedures are
characterized by the use of the simple past tense usually with time
adverbials, the opening is a list, while the conclusion is a comparative statement.

This account of various text types is based on work developed in
Australia (see Christie 1989 and also Swales 1990). The work has
provoked a great deal of controversy with people taking up en-
trenched positions on both sides. Opponents of this genre approach
believe it encourages a formulaic attitude to writing; advocates
believe it offers the best way to involve pupils in creating the types
of texts that lead to full participation in modern society. I do not
wish to enter into these debates, except to observe that the enterprise of trying to describe the basic structures and linguistic configurations of, admittedly, simple texts is potentially very helpful to
teachers. To prove its worth fully, the work needs to be extended
to a wider range of texts and to texts that serve more complex

functions. How teachers use the knowledge is, of course, an important pedagogic issue and one that is discussed in the next two sections. Knowledge of text structures does not in any way entail teaching pupils inflexible strategies; it does provide a basis for offering help that is systematic both in the process of developing a text and in the assessment of the product when that is required. It also helps to ensure a balanced approach to the writing curriculum in which, for example, narrative is not seen as the most or only favoured form.

In the next section, there is a discussion of how to set about writing which includes some planning devices that will help pupils gain control over the types of writing described in this section.

SUMMARY

- It is not easy to determine the range of writing that should be developed in schools. However, traditional forms, such as the essay, are not normally practised in society. There is a danger in developing forms that are only school-specific.
- A writing task has to be seen in relation to a purpose, a form (or text type) and an audience or readership. In setting writing tasks, teachers need to make these matters clear to pupils.
- Developing an understanding of how texts are organized is an important aspect of the teaching of writing.

3 Approaches to writing

For a fortunate few, writing is a quickly achieved objective. Most of us, however, find that writing is full of starts and stops, punctuated by long pauses for reflection or by the need to regenerate concentration. The work may also require a lot of reworking or revising before we feel at all satisfied with the result.

The last twenty years have seen great steps forward in our understanding of the processes of writing and in our realization that these processes can be harnessed to help learner writers. We are also beginning to realize that the development of certain ways of approaching the whole task of writing – writing behaviour – is an important aspect of teaching successful writing.

In this section, then, I will look first at the processes of writing and, secondly, at writing behaviours.

3.1 The processes of writing

Most of our understanding of the processes of writing has been gathered from accounts by professional writers of how they go about their tasks. To this introspective evidence, we can now add some more systematic observations of how pupils and college students approach writing (Emig 1971, Pianko 1979). There are clear indications of general patterns in the processes, but we should also be aware that individuals differ. Classroom practice, therefore, should never become so systematic and routine that it allows no room for individual differences.

It is usual to consider the processes of writing in three stages:

pre-writing; drafting; revising and editing. There are, however, some problems with this simple classification. The first stage, pre-writing, may well involve writing in one form or another; and the second and third stages will often in reality merge and become intertwined. Granted the tendency for these to run into each other and to overlap, I find it useful to think of the processes in three stages, although I prefer to use different terms which indicate more precisely the nature of the activities likely to occur at each stage.

3.1.1 Stage 1 – assembling strategies

Any piece of writing requires some thought before committing pen to paper. Even if it is something as informal as a casual note, some thought is necessary. With more formal and extended tasks this first stage is almost certain to be prolonged. We need time to sort out or develop ideas. We may need time to read or undertake other forms of research (in a library or in the field conducting interviews, for instance). We may need time to talk to other people at length in order to test ideas, to clarify our thoughts or to gain necessary information.

It is worth stressing the importance of this first stage because it is usually either neglected or made into a routine of prescriptive planning or **brainstorming**. I have had several experiences that testify to the importance of this stage of assembling and clarifying ideas. Once, several years ago, I was mulling over an idea for a short story. The idea originally occurred to me as a picture – rather like a still from a film – but the picture would not become animated. Several weeks passed with the image hovering in my mind and various ideas developing but being rejected as false. Then, one night, as I was walking home late, the whole concept came to life and I wrote the story that same night in a matter of hours. It needed revising subsequently, but only in detail. The 'assembling' stage had lasted, on and off, for over a month while the next stage of 'creating the text' took only a few hours. I have had similar experiences with different types of writing and do not believe that the process varies in any fundamental way from one sort of writing to another.

However, it is quite obvious that in classroom practice no one can wait around for several weeks while ideas for writing slowly come to fruition. We need strategies that will help pupils, but in an accelerated fashion. This, then, is the purpose of assembling strategies.

Many techniques have been developed over the last few years that help pupils to assemble ideas. I have already mentioned talking to others (informal chats or structured discussions), reading and undertaking research. Here are some further suggestions that are all tried and tested in both L1 and L2 writing contexts.

Listing questions

This is a simple, effective but neglected technique. It helps writers get a sense of the task in hand and provides a focus for research which can include reading and simple fact-finding activities. With inexperienced writers this listing can be done as a group/class activity with the teacher acting as the secretary to the group, noting down the suggestions offered by the pupils. The procedure can prove useful as a preliminary part of topic work or before an educational visit, for example.

A useful extension is to create two lists – what is already known and what needs to be found out. A simple planning sheet can assist, with two headings as follows:

What I know	What I need to know

Underlying this apparently simple procedure are two important points about learning:

— We learn most effectively by linking new knowledge and understanding into our existing frameworks, which are in due course modified by this new knowledge and understanding.

— For learning to be effective, we need to be in control of the process as far as we can be by becoming aware at a conscious level of just what we do, in fact, know or understand about the subject. It is often the case that techniques like listing are needed to bring such awareness to the threshold of our consciousness.

As with other techniques described later, this listing procedure can be used with various writing 'technologies'. Obviously, it is a simple matter to make copies of planning sheets for pupils to use (an example can be seen in action in chapter 5). White or black boards are useful when working with a class or group, but any large sheets of paper are perfectly adequate. Use can also be made of simple computer applications if appropriate.

Brainstorming

This technique of jotting down words and phrases in a free association manner has become very popular; but there is a danger that the technique can be over-used without any real understanding of its strengths and weaknesses. At best, because there is no pressure to fit ideas together into a pattern or to worry about relevance, it can unlock a flow of thought, particularly if the writer is experiencing a 'block'. It can also be adapted to many different purposes. Although the technique has become popular in topic or project work at primary level, it is also possible to use it to develop character, ideas for the plot or details of the setting for a narrative. It has a place, too, in science and technology work. It should be borne in mind that this technique, like others described in this section, need not be restricted to contexts where writing is the eventual outcome. Brainstorming can be a fruitful preliminary to a group discussion, for example.

However, brainstorming does have drawbacks. Writing blocks are usually associated with having no ideas – hence the common cry that as teachers we are well accustomed to: 'I haven't any ideas' or 'I don't know what to say'. It is also the case that having a lot of ideas that do not fall into a pattern can be inhibiting. Brainstorming, therefore, needs to be used with caution and a second stage following a brainstorm may well be necessary in the assembling process to ensure a reasonable chance of a successful outcome. A simple, but effective second-stage procedure is to review the product of a brainstorming session and invite pupils to create links between ideas/keywords: when using a whiteboard or a large sheet of paper these links can be colour-coded.

Diagrams

If pupils have ideas but need to organize them – if they have just completed a brainstorm, for instance – it can be useful to suggest that they sort out their ideas through the use of a diagram. A common form of diagram is a flow-chart in which the progression of ideas is plotted.

Another form of diagram that incorporates a controlled type of brainstorm is a 'mind map'. This technique was first developed as a computer application.

In the example on page 50, created by a group of 10-year-olds, the task is to consider ideas for improving the local environment. The main categories are the ringed headings *LITTER*, *DOGS* and so on. Under each heading more specific ideas are included which can subsequently be incorporated into a piece of writing, or, indeed, many other kinds of presentations and activities such as devising posters for a clean-up campaign.

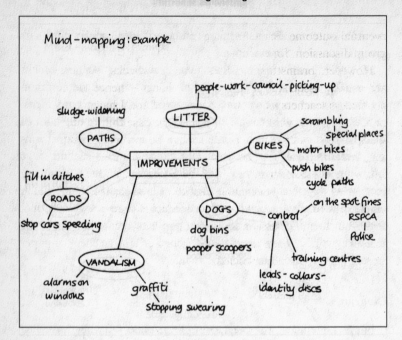

Mind-mapping: example

people-work-council-picking-up

LITTER

sludge-widening

PATHS

IMPROVEMENTS

BIKES

scrambling
special places
motor bikes
push bikes
cycle paths

fill in ditches

ROADS

stop cars speeding

DOGS

control

on the spot fines
RSPCA
Police

dog bins
pooper scoopers

training centres

leads - collars -
identity discs

VANDALISM

alarms on
windows

graffiti

stopping swearing

Planning grids

Earlier in this chapter I described how questions could be developed
into two lists *What I know* and *What I need to know*. In a similar
way there are many planning grids that can help pupils in the
assembling stages of writing. The seven grids presented on pages
51–2 have been found useful.

The first four grids are most obviously useful in developing points
of view and arguments – both difficult forms of writing because
they require writers to be able to organize their ideas into an
appropriate sequence. Grids 5 and 6 are rather more sophisticated
planning grids that also help in these sorts of writing.

The last example of a planning grid (7) is designed for use when a
comparison is being made.

Approaches to writing

GRID 1	
For	Against

GRID 2		
Fact	Opinion	Not sure

GRID 3		
Agree	Disagree	Don't know

GRID 4	
If I say . . .	They will say . . .

GRID 5
In my opinion Good points   Bad points From other materials and sources Good points   Bad points

GRID 6
What are your views? I agree that . . . I don't think that . . . I feel strongly that . . . In my opinion . . .

GRID 7		
Feature	Object A	Object B

Making a comparison is not simply a matter of matching one object against another; it is a matter of matching two things against each other in certain respects. There are, then, always three aspects at least to be held in mind – the quality or feature, object A and object B. Making comparisons is recognized as a complex intellectual activity; the means by which comparisons are expressed in writing is also complex linguistically (see Harris and Wilkinson 1986, Hoey 1983 and Winter 1977). However, with the help of a planning grid, even young pupils can begin to get to grips with this sort of writing.

Planning stories

All the planning techniques described so far are more appropriate to non-narrative writing than to story writing. However, narratives can also be planned to some extent; and it is a good thing to encourage young writers to do so since, without an initial plan (no matter if it is later modified), stories can easily become out of balance and sections out of proportion to the whole. In chapter 2 the general features of narratives were set out and the following planning ideas are based on those analyses of story structure (see, particularly, the activity on page 26).

STORY PLANNER

The first planning sheet takes the notion of 'setting' and 'problems' and 'solutions' with a 'resolution' at the end.

Setting – who and where?

Story trigger – what sets your story going?

Problems and solutions – episodes leading to . . .

Outcome – the conclusion of the story

STORYBOARD

Another popular device is the storyboard. This can be a series of sketches with or without notes, as follows:

Who? Where?	What begins the story?	How does it develop?	How does it end?
Notes	Notes	Notes	Notes

Drawing can, in fact, be a fruitful form of assembling ideas, particularly with young writers.

STORY TREE

Finally, a story tree can be used to combine the planning of the setting (the 'who?' 'what?' 'where?') with the action (the events or episodes that go to make up the narrative sequence).

Setting		
Who?	Where?	How it starts
Episodes	1.	
	2.	
	3.	
	4.	
Conclusion		

I have put a great deal of emphasis on the first stage of the writing process because in many classrooms it is the most neglected aspect. Even in classrooms where drafting is a normal practice, pupils are often expected to plunge straight into their first draft without any prior thought or plan. Writers need time to get their thoughts together and into a pattern. Exploratory discussions, reading and other forms of research are all important and need to be given a positive emphasis. More closely focused support can then be given through the use of appropriate planning grids/sheets. It is important to stress to pupils that planning sheets and brainstorming do not require perfectly correct and perfectly formed writing. Speed is of the essence and accuracy is not important at this stage of the process.

3.1.2   Stage 2 – creating and developing the text

The next stage of the writing process is to translate plans and ideas into a provisional text. It is often the case that the most difficult part of a piece of writing is the opening, particularly of a formal report or essay. Drafting allows a writer to start with whatever part of the projected whole comes most easily. I have found both when writing myself and when working with pupils that it can help to simply say to oneself or to them, 'Get something down corresponding to a part of your plan and then see how you feel about it.' This is a way of overcoming that awful sense of paralysis, of staring at a blank piece of paper and not knowing how to begin. If pupils are word-processing, this technique works perfectly well, provided that they know how to manipulate blocks using the 'cut and paste' commands. Similarly with pen and paper, sections can be cut out and moved around provided that the writing is done on loose sheets of paper and not in exercise books – which, incidentally, are anathema to the development of good writing habits.

It is often the case that as writers proceed with creating a text they come to redefine ideas, perceive a different and more significant way of sequencing their ideas, think of new ideas and new linkages between ideas and, indeed, may even change their minds over a point of view or argument. In this sense writing can be an act of discovery – that is one of its excitements! However, this means that the text as it is being created has to be seen as provisional. One of the biggest drawbacks of traditional 'one-shot' writing is that it can inhibit or distort thinking because what is once written cannot be changed even if the writer has lost confidence in it. In contrast, drafting allows writers the flexibility to explore, to make discoveries and to change their ideas.

Once a first version has been created, changes and revisions may be needed. Bits of text can be deleted, added or moved to a different place – that, in essence, is what the physical act of revising is all about. It is the quality of perception that informs these decisions that is all important. We need to offer pupils strategies for making changes that will relieve them as far as possible of the daunting task of writing and rewriting.

The actual creating of a text is, for most writers, a process that demands a great deal of concentration and application. It is, therefore, understandable that pupils will feel resistant if, once the initial draft is done, the next demand is for another draft. This will not only be seen as a rejection of what has already been achieved but the very thought of having to do more writing will in itself affect motivation adversely. As teachers (and collaborators) we should always be on our guard that when suggesting alterations we are not imposing our own style, ideas or preferred wording on someone else's text. Young and inexperienced writers do not need this sort of 'school-masterly' interference; rather they need sympathetic readers who will enter into their way of seeing and expressing things.

The first essential in establishing techniques for revising is to look for ways to reduce the amount of physical rewriting that is required in a second or subsequent draft. If the initial draft has been word-processed, the revising is not so irksome and time-consuming. With pen and paper there is a danger that pupils will see drafting as simply a punitive exercise involving massive amounts of writing and rewriting. A friend who had visited one of the centres of 'process writing' in the USA told me a true horror story about a 10-year-old who was writing his fourth draft on a science topic. My friend asked to see the earlier drafts. Each was identical. Puzzled, she asked if he had kept his initial notes. No, he explained, he had no notes because his first draft had been copied out of a text-book! This is an example of how drafting can become a mindless imposition which is not only no better than 'one-shot' writing but positively worse since it involves four or five times the amount of writing – if, that is, there is no sense of genuine text development.

One way to reduce the burden of rewriting is to create conditions in which pupils are free to use 'cut and paste' techniques quite literally. Initial drafts should be written on separate sheets of paper (one side only) so that the revising process can be an assemblage of the sections of the text that are approved by the writer with minor changes written over and any major alterations written out on another sheet of paper ready to stick into the right place. The whole text can then be pasted up on a larger sheet of paper. In this way the physical process of revising becomes enjoyable and does not seem like writing but more like play!

If pupils have to use exercise books for their writing the 'cut and paste' technique is not appropriate. However, the burden of rewriting can be reduced by using parallel pages – draft text on the right-hand page and revisions entered on the left-hand page. It will also help to give pupils a range of editing/revising markers such as asterisks, arrows and insertion marks.

It will be obvious that these techniques for reducing the amount of rewriting do not produce neat and beautifully written scripts. However, I am convinced that we need to change our attitudes to writing in schools in a quite fundamental way in relation to the question of presentation. Writing is a messy process. Considering the process as a whole I see a dual progression in the physical and the intellectual aspects. Just as our thoughts and ideas begin to achieve a coherence and a clarity as we move from initial jottings and plans through drafts and revisions to the final product, so the physical look of what we write is likely to be a gradual emergence of order from chaos – of something ordered and of a high quality in its presentation arising out of the disorder of crossings out, insertions and scribbled additions written above, below or to the side of the text.

Revising a draft, however, is not just a matter of randomly cutting and pasting and making word changes. Such techniques are only the means to an end and will be quite useless, even harmful, if writers do not understand how and why they can improve their writing. The most obvious starting point for helping a writer improve his or her text is to act as a reader. To be a supportive reader requires a great deal of tact and skill. It is important not to impose on the writer but rather to try to understand the writer's intentions and to try to help fulfil these. With pupils who are not used to acting as readers of each other's work it will be found best to group them into threes. This avoids a one-to-one situation with the in-built possibility of confrontation. To emphasize that being a good reader of a draft is not an exercise in negative criticism, readers should be asked to identify two or three points that they particularly like and also two or three points where they feel development or changes are appropriate. In all this work it is vital that both the writers and the readers should be developing their awareness of text types so that their criticisms and comments are based on a sound understanding of the sort of text that is being constructed. This is an area in which the teacher should play an important role in developing the perceptions of the pupils.

3.1.3 Stage 3 – editing

It is sometimes said that a piece of writing is never finished; it is simply released and not worked on further – a process called publication! This is said because we recognize that a text is always capable of further revision and also because a text is recreated with different emphases and interpretations each time it is read. Although there is an important general truth in this, in classroom contexts there has to be a moment when a writer decides that the text is complete. The decision may be a pragmatic compromise with the demands of deadlines, the limits of perseverance or even a sense that there is nothing more that can be done to improve what is already there – revisions do not inevitably improve a text, after all! Particularly with young writers, there is no point in forcing the issue since to do so could set up negative reactions to writing.

When the decision is made that the draft is finished there remains the task of editing and publishing. Editing involves the careful checking of the text to ensure that there are no errors that will impede communication – errors of spelling, punctuation, word choice and word order. Skilful writers know that they need to read a text carefully. However, this is not a naturally acquired habit. It is something that needs to be taught. With young and inexperienced writers encouragement to acquire this habit can be given by arranging for pairs of pupils to work together on a text written by one of them. This sharing of the work helps to keep motivation and concentration at a high level. Establishing this approach to editing in the classroom will create a much more positive attitude than the traditional method of the teacher correcting pupils' texts. It encourages the self-help and independence from the teacher that are necessary attributes of mature and confident writers.

Publishing pupils' work used to be a routine matter of mounting work for display on the walls of the classroom, often too high up for pupils to be able to read in comfort, if at all. Although wall displays are a legitimate way of publishing pupils' writing if care is taken in placing the displays, there are other means that should be used at least some of the time. Pupils can be encouraged to make simple individual books of their writing, illustrating the cover and some inside pages. These books should then be made available for others to read in a reading or quiet corner. Another method is to create a class book in which every pupil's piece of writing is included. The class book should be made available in an area of the classroom and time scheduled so that individuals or groups can share the writing of their peers. Needless to say, displays of early drafts alongside finished products will give a legitimacy to the practice of drafting.

As a summary of the main stages of the writing process, a diagram that shows these stages and the kinds of classroom activities that might accompany them is presented opposite.

3.2 Writing behaviours

Hand in hand with giving pupils access to the processes of writing should be a developing awareness of the kinds of behaviour that will enhance the possibilities of success and satisfaction in writing. A helpful summary of research into writing behaviour is provided by Krashen (1984). He highlights three particular areas where there is a difference between the habits of good and poor writers.

3.2.1 Planning

Studies show that good writers plan more than poor writers, spending more time reflecting, thinking or making notes before creating a first draft. Good writers also tend to be more flexible in their approaches to planning, using a variety of techniques, whereas poor writers are likely to adhere rigidly to one method of planning no matter whether it is helpful to them or to the task in hand. They are also unlikely to revise an initial plan, seeing writing as an endeavour to fulfil the plan and no more, while good writers are likely to revise their plans as they proceed.

Approaches to writing

THE WRITING PROCESS	
Stages of the writing process	**Classroom activities**
1. Assembling strategies	Listing questions Brainstorming Research (including reading and note-making) Diagrams Planning (using grids and planning sheets) Considering text type, purpose and readership
2. Creating and developing the text	Drafting using 'cut and paste' techniques for revising text Provisional responses from readers (teacher and response-partners) Reconsidering text type, purpose and readership
3. Editing	Making a final draft Careful reading/proof-reading of text Publication

Note It should be borne in mind that the activities listed under Classroom activities represent possibilities from which a selection can be made. It should also be remembered that in reality the process of producing a written text is never so schematically neat as can be shown in a diagram.

3.2.2 Revising

In this aspect of writing the contrast is striking. While good writers are likely to make changes to the content, organization and wording of their texts, poor writers tend to make few alterations beyond correcting spelling and punctuation. In this sense they do not enter genuinely into the process of drafting and revising; they see it merely as an act of editing.

3.2.3 Rescanning

This is Krashen's term for reading back over the text so far developed – whether this is only part of a draft or a full draft. Good writers have been observed to pause more while writing as they scan back along what they have already written to ensure that the text is maintaining an overall **coherence**. Poor writers, in contrast, rarely review or scan back even when a draft is finished.

Although Krashen's summary may contain nothing particularly surprising, it is important to note the differences and accept that teachers need to encourage the less successful writers to acquire better habits. Teachers often complain to me that their pupils do not read back over what they have just written and, as a consequence, leave out words or even lose the thread of what they are writing. When I ask them if they teach their pupils to read back as part of the whole approach to writing the answer is usually negative.

There is a place for directly teaching skills such as rescanning. There is also a place for the indirect teaching of good writing habits. This can be done through 'modelling', where the teacher sometimes writes with a group or in sight of the pupils, as suggested in the UK National Curriculum requirements for English. It can also be achieved through the way in which the classroom is managed and in the expectations about writing that are communicated to the pupils.

SUMMARY

- Writing is a process that usually involves several stages. Pupils need to have experience of this process and to develop their own approach to writing accordingly. However, the process of writing should not become a rigid system that specifies a given number of stages or drafts.
- There are certain ways of 'behaving' as a writer that are helpful. These include, for example, reading back while developing a text. Teachers should not expect such skills to develop naturally. They need to be taught, at least through example.

4 Writing in the classroom

4.1 Setting writing tasks

In chapter 2, I suggested that the specific nature of a writing task was formed by a combination of factors in which the purpose, form and readership were of crucial importance – purpose here used to indicate the writer's communicative intentions. There is another sense in which purpose is important to the writing curriculum – that is, the reason why a pupil undertakes or is asked to undertake a writing task.

Traditionally, the question 'Why write?' has been answered in L1 contexts by pointing to the need to see if some area of knowledge has been understood; and to practise and develop the ability to create the sort of texts on which public assessments are based and which form the staple diet of higher education (essays, for instance). More recently, the answer has been couched in terms of personal development. Writing, in this sense, is seen as a way of expressing the self and discovering through the act of writing something more of one's individuality and social identity.

In L2 contexts, writing is often seen as a means of practising the grammar, vocabulary and discourse structures of the target language, particularly where the target language is the medium of instruction in the education system or, more commonly, in higher education.

In short, there are both instrumental and personal purposes for writing in school. These need to be given due weight, but should not be so much taken for granted that we neglect to ask ourselves what is the aim of the activity each time we set up a writing situation.

4.1.1 Purpose as perceived by writer

In chapter 1 I suggested a unique relationship between writing and ways of thinking. If we put this together with other justifications for writing we can define four main purposes, as follows:
— communicating and sharing experiences
— constructing meanings through ways of thinking not usually available through speaking
— discovering and clarifying thoughts (which can also be a function of talk)
— providing a record of ideas, facts and experiences in a form that allows them to be worked on, organized, referred back to and developed subsequently.

Often, more than one of these reasons will be present in a writing activity. The important point is that a writing task should have a clear justification and one that is understood by the pupils. If not, the chances of a successful outcome will be jeopardized and over a period of time pupils are likely to lose motivation towards their writing.

ACTIVITY

Consider the aims of writing in your classroom. List them as honestly as you can. Then list what you think your pupils' perceptions about writing and the aims of writing are. If you are able to collect some opinions through a questionnaire, so much the better.

In the early stages of the National Writing Project in England and Wales, pupils' attitudes to writing were widely canvassed through a variety of means – questionnaires, interviews and so on. It came as something of a shock to many teachers to see how pupils regarded writing. Some examples that we collected in our local part of the project in Sheffield in response to the question 'What is writing for?' are:

— *You have to write. If you didn't there'd be no point in going to school.*

— *So's the teacher knows you've been working.*

— *Don't know really. Probably just for school.*

— *It's to fill up all the time we have at school.*

— *To show it to Miss when it's done.*

— *To learn joined up letters and how to spell.*

(Examples taken from Stallard 1988)

All these pupils were under 10 years old – which goes to show how quickly they had learned that schools can be writing factories or sweat-shops! More seriously, when we appreciate the perceptions that some pupils have of the writing that they have to do in schools, it should make us realize the need for clarity about why we ask them to write.

4.1.2 Purpose as perceived by teacher

At the centre of this issue of aims and purposes is the procedure by which writing tasks or assignments are determined. And to go a step further, there is also the question whether we should be thinking at all about writing tasks rather than about learning tasks in which writing has a part to play. This distinction may be best explained through typical examples.

Writing as an imposed topic

In this model of writing no matter how carefully the lead-up is structured and no matter how strongly pupils are encouraged to use a 'process' approach, the control of the writing topic remains with the teacher. If the chosen topic happens to strike a sympathetic chord with some of the pupils that is fortunate, but it is unlikely that it will appeal to all the class.

Writing as the end-point of learning

This model is frequently the only one that pupils experience. At primary level it characteristically takes the form of having to write about a visit or activity – often, it would appear, simply so that there is a record of the pupil having been on the visit. The visit may have been enjoyable; the writing makes it educational. At secondary level this model of writing predominates in many subject areas. After several lessons exploring the religions of the world represented in the classroom, for example, there comes the instruction to write about the major world faiths!

Writing as integral to learning

In this model, writing is seen as one of several means to facilitate learning. The content and focus of the learning take priority over writing but, with careful planning, writing in a variety of forms and for a variety of purposes can play a vital part in supporting and advancing the learning. Writing in this model can also be a means to an end other than writing itself. It may be an aid to discussion or to a graphic presentation, for instance.

Writing as an aesthetic artefact

There is a particular place in the writing curriculum for aesthetic uses of writing. Playing with words and word patterns such as rhymes and jingles, with forms and structures such as repetitive stories and many types of jokes, provides a continuity with the world of literature. Even in this model – which is not strictly in competition with the others already described – there are different approaches which indicate something about the control over the writing that occurs in the classroom. According to one approach, topics and titles may be suggested by the teacher: the subject matter is under control and there is no attention to structure and form. More challenging is an approach which establishes a form that can be explored for its possibilities with the choice of subject matter being left to the individual. This sort of approach can occur only if teaching has created an awareness of formal elements – in the way that I described for narrative in chapter 2.

Fundamental to all these models is the question of control, which I have already touched upon. There are three possibilities: the teacher controls the writing task; the teacher hands over control to the pupils; teacher and pupils together negotiate to determine and refine the writing task. It seems to me that the third approach is most likely to motivate pupils. This approach may not always be possible, and sometimes not even desirable, but it should serve as the standard.

4.2   Developing writing in the early stages

I chose to start this section on writing in the classroom with a discussion of the aims of writing and with comments on pupils' perceptions because attitudes to writing are developed very early on. It is, therefore, important that early experiences of writing are framed in such a way that pupils feel positive about the activity. They are likely to feel positive if they receive support, are able to create meanings for themselves and are not inhibited by a fear of making mistakes. Evidence comes from studies of both L1 and L2 writers to show that success is marked most by an understanding of the nature of writing and how to approach the activity. In other words, pupils develop into good writers by virtue of their attitude to writing and their understanding of the processes, irrespective of the stage of development they have reached in their command of the language. To enable the fostering of positive attitudes teachers need to be clear about goals and priorities.

To establish the creation and communication of meaning as the primary aim of writing from the beginning has radical implications for the classroom. Any form of sentence-completion exercise or the filling in of blanks in given sentences, for instance, gives a pupil no sense whatsoever that the creation of meaning has a priority. Responses from teachers that concentrate solely on errors inevitably lead pupils to the point of view that writing is not about creating meaning but about getting it right! Writing activities that consist of copying what the teacher has written also reinforce the notion that writing is about correct presentation (in this case, handwriting skills) rather than the creation of meaning.

Yet we have to face the fact that when beginning to learn to write there are many things that have to be learned just to get started. Support can be given in a variety of ways. I shall describe three which have been found effective by teachers working with L1 and L2 writers.

4.2.1 Resource banks

One way is by providing words and phrases from which pupils can make individual selections. *Breakthrough to Literacy* is a commercially produced set of resources which incorporates this approach. Even if it is not possible to purchase the apparatus, the basic strategy can be employed using resources made by the teacher. Carefully selected banks of word-cards reflecting anticipated themes and topics, along with phrase cards that provide a range of useful structures, will give pupils the chance to create their own texts either in groups, pairs or individually. On page 70 is an example of words and phrases used with 6-year-olds on the theme of shopping after a shop had been set up in the home corner.

From this assortment of words and phrases it can be seen that a wide range of short texts can be constructed. If a pupil wishes to use a word that is not in the prepared bank the teacher can easily provide it if he or she has a stock of blank cards to hand.

The drawback of this approach is that it takes a lot of preparation and needs careful classroom management. It is best used with only one group at a time, assuming that group work is the normal form of classroom organization. Storage needs to be considered carefully and routines worked out systematically. Pupils also need space to spread out their words and phrases. Research has shown,

I went to the	shops	and
	supermarket	but
	market	it
	toyshop	they
	bookshop	
	drugstore	

			cost
I bought	a	any	dollars
	some	enough	pounds (etc)
	one		
	two (etc)		

a packet of	bread	meat
packets of	rice	fish
a bottle of	flour	vegetables
bottles of		
a piece of		
a book about		
pencils		
felt-tips		
a games machine		

| I had | | |
| I didn't have. | | |

(Author's Data)

however, that the actual physical handling of the words and phrases can lead to an enhancement of memory. This is particularly valuable when working with young L2 learners or any pupil who has a limited memory span. *Breakthrough to Literacy*, for example, has been found effective with lower secondary pupils who have not progressed far with their writing because they cannot hold words in their memories and have become disillusioned with the whole activity of writing.

4.2.2 Collaborative approach

The teacher can set up a collaboration with the pupils. In this approach the teacher acts as 'scribe' or secretary for a group of pupils or, on occasions, for an individual pupil (though this is time-consuming and can lead to both teacher and pupil being content with a one-sentence text, such as a caption accompanying a picture). There are several ways to use this collaborative strategy for early writing. A small whiteboard that can be managed while sitting down with pupils grouped around is useful, particularly since alterations to the developing text can be made easily – thus setting up a model of the provisionality of creating text. It is also perfectly adequate to use any large sheets of paper. A third technique is to use large sheets of acetate with the appropriate water-based pens or markers. The sheets can be cleaned and used time after time. A specific advantage of this technique is that the sheets of acetate can be clipped to a card base on which a planning grid has been prepared. A commercial scheme that uses this approach is *Reasons for Writing – early stages* (Harris and Sanderson 1989).

One of the great benefits of this type of group work is the opportunities that it provides for encouraging positive attitudes to the process of writing – discussing choices, making changes, reading back over the text as it develops and so on; it also sets up opportunities for reflecting on both the process and the text itself. Encouraging pupils to reflect on what they have achieved is an important but neglected aspect of developing positive attitudes to writing and learning.

4.2.3 Emergent or developmental writing

The third approach is the most radical, but is strongly advocated by teachers who have adopted it. It is sometimes called 'Emergent Writing', sometimes 'Developmental Writing'. The relative merits of these two labels is not of importance since both indicate that the approach stresses growth towards capability as a writer, with the emphasis always on the creation of meaning. The means by which meaning is constructed may appear to be unconventional and even idiosyncratic – invented symbols, pictures, combinations of letters, symbols and words from both the mother tongue and the target language and so on. This means, of course, that in these early stages the teacher may need to help communicate the writer's intention to other pupils. Experience, however, has shown that pupils who learn to compose using this approach have a strong motivation to acquire the conventional forms of writing in the target language. The following activity illustrates this approach.

ACTIVITY

Here are two texts constructed by pupils using the variety of means described just now. What meaning can you perceive in them?

The first (text 4a) is by a 6-year-old native English speaker, Richard. This is a 'translation' of Richard's letter:

Dear Father Christmas,
Please will you bring me a Transformer.
How are your reindeer?
love from
Richard

Richard uses a variety of methods for creating his message. The opening address to Father Christmas and the signing off are conventional but were given by the teacher. In the main part of his letter he uses phonetic approximations (spelling as he hears or sounds the word) – *pliz*, *wil*, *mi*. Sometimes he uses what appear to be shortened forms of visually remembered words – *y* for *you*, *p* for *bring* (possibly because he was trying to write a *b*), *hr* for *how* and *yr* for *your*. When the word he wishes to use is long and/or complicated he uses a sketch to indicate his meaning – *transformer* and *reindeer*.

72

4a

LINC data

The second – taken from Savva (1990) – is by a Cantonese native speaker, Wan Leong, who is learning to learn in English. In this first draft he combines his knowledge of both Cantonese and English to create his message.

4b

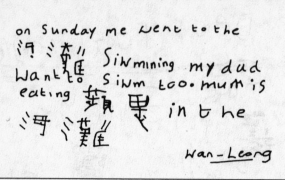

Wan Leong later rewrote his text using English throughout.

4c

On Sunday I went to the
Sea-Side to siwm my dad want
to Siwm tcc mum is eating
an apple at the Sea-Side and I
Just siwm.

These are just two of many examples from case studies that show
how effectively this approach to writing works in the hands of
thoughtful teachers. Development towards communication in the
conventional orthography does not, of course, occur as if by
magic. Teachers will use many supporting strategies to facilitate
that development. I will briefly mention some of these under the
general heading of the classroom environment for writing.

4.3 The classroom environment for writing in the early stages

4.3.1 Sharing stories and other types of writing

If I had to make a choice of the single most important factor in creating a good environment for writing, I would without hesitation name the sharing of stories and other types of writing. In good early-years teaching the importance of sharing stories, poems and rhymes is acknowledged. More could be done to extend the range of text types shared in this way. Through hearing, enjoying and reflecting upon what they have shared, pupils assimilate the structures of the texts at both a macro and a micro level – not only vocabulary items, but sentence and discourse structures. Needless to say, good quality texts also present pupils with good language models unlike the purpose-written basal readers that are all too often the only models presented to pupils, particularly in L2 contexts. These readers use bogus language forms such as the present tense for narrative because the text is linked to a series of pictures and because there is an unquestioned belief that for L2 pupils learning the present tense is somehow easier than the past tense, although some research has indicated that this is not the case. It is true that newer L2 readers avoid such extremes of artificiality.

4.3.2 Sharing each other's writing

I have stressed that writers need people to read their drafts and they need to know about their readership. Acquiring this knowledge is a long-term aim of teaching writing. A start, however, can be made in the early stages. A good writing classroom will be one where pupils are encouraged to share their writing with each other, both at draft and final product stage. Opportunities need to be built into the structure of the session.

Thought should also be given to the question of how best to present pupils' writing. Rather than the traditional wall-mounted displays which are often difficult or impossible for pupils to read, it is much better to create 'Big Books' in which pupils' writing is mounted. These can be placed in a quiet area set aside for reading or they can be taken to a table for sharing by a group of pupils.

4.3.3 Writing areas

Many teachers have found that spending some time and effort on creating 'writing areas' pays great dividends in the motivation it gives pupils. These areas can be integrated with an activity area or 'home corner' to establish a focus for writing – for example, a restaurant, a hair salon, a surgery or a travel agency. Appropriate forms such as appointments diaries, booking forms, menus and so on – can be placed in the area. Pupils may not be able to do more than scribble-write on the forms but this in itself will give them a sense of communicating, of using writing for a variety of purposes and of creating a variety of texts. It adds a writing dimension to their structured play.

In writing areas it is useful to provide, if resources allow, a variety of implements for writing and a variety of types and sizes of paper. One box of scrap paper could be labelled 'for rough work' and another 'for best'. This will help pupils to realize from early on that there are different writing behaviours appropriate to different stages of the writing process and to different sorts of texts. It is generally acknowledged that pupils need to develop a range of strategies for reading; we should also be developing a range of similar strategies for writing.

The writing area can also be used to help develop a sense of text types. Some teachers have found that displaying carefully selected texts in the area helps to build up pupils' awareness of text differences. For instance, a recipe can be contrasted with a story, a set of instructions with a counting rhyme. The texts should not just be placed in the area; they need to be introduced by the teacher and pupils should then be encouraged to discuss them with each other. Opportunities for group or class discussion should also be created: these will consolidate individuals' perceptions.

4.4   Writing development

As I indicated in chapter 2, formal, large-scale research has concentrated on identifying features of writing that can be counted (quantifiable measures) and, by applying these to a body of pupils' writing, has sought to establish norms of attainment at different stages of schooling. The quantifiable measures used in these studies include the overall length of texts, average sentence length, the frequency and variety of subordination and the incidence of personal pronouns.

There are several problems with the basic assumptions of this quantifiable approach to describing writing development. The language features isolated for study are problematic. For instance, the incidence of relative clauses is taken as one indicator of development. It is, however, difficult to maintain that *Tom sailed his submarine which is yellow* is more complex than *Tom sailed his yellow submarine*. We would need to know in context whether the two versions were expressing the same meaning or whether 'the one which is yellow' is to be distinguished from, say, 'the one which is grey'.

A second reservation that is acknowledged by some of the researchers themselves is that the approach appears valid for describing only the early stages of development – up to the age of 13.

A third problem is that little account has been taken in any of the studies of variations in text types. Harpin (1976) alone makes any distinction. He uses a simple division of texts into the categories of 'factual' and 'creative' that reflects the practice in primary classrooms in England at the time of his study.

Nevertheless, despite the limitations of these studies there are in them some basic indications about development that we should not ignore. I shall group comments under three headings which, subsequently, will be related to classroom practices that are designed to facilitate writing development.

4.4.1 Cognitive development

Writing development can be seen in part as an aspect of generally increasing knowledge and cognitive ability.

This may appear to be an obvious starting point. Yet it is important to realize that one explanation for the increasing length of pupils' texts is simply that they know and have experienced more and therefore have more to write about. Nobody can generalize successfully about something on the basis of only one experience of that thing, whatever it is. And it is a well-documented feature of mother-tongue development that young children create general hypotheses about classes of objects, such as four-legged creatures, which they successively modify as their experience widens. At another level of learning, the ability to conceptualize develops from being able to draw upon a wide range of instances and also from being able to perceive patterns within and between these instances. Clearly these aspects of development are not only or even primarily related to writing development; but it is equally clear that they will have a significant impact on writing itself. Indeed, in turn, the act of writing may well be a major influence on the development of these abilities, as I indicated in chapter 1.

A similar aspect of general development that affects writing has been noted by Moffett (1968). He identifies a feature which he calls 'decentring': by this he means the ability to move from a focus on how something affects you personally to a focus on the thing itself. Again, it is necessary to exercise caution before regarding this as in any sense an absolute statement of development. Much will depend on the contexts created, the tasks set up and the expectations communicated. For all that, this aspect of development is likely to be revealed in the increasing ability to determine relevance, to make principled selections and orderings of information and to evaluate what has been undertaken through reflection on both the processes of writing and on the eventual product.

4.4.2 Writing and 'writerly language'

A second important aspect of development as a writer will involve a pupil moving from uses of language that are like those of speech to those that are more specifically appropriate to the written mode. In chapter 1 a detailed comparison was made between speech and writing. It will, therefore, be sufficient here to summarize some of the main aspects of development that show this progression from speech-like to 'writerly' uses of language.

Kress (1982) in an important study shows that speech typically tends to employ co-ordinating or chaining constructions, while writing tends to employ hierarchically organized structures with embedding at several different levels. This process of embedding is most characteristically seen in the use of subordinate clauses. This is not to endorse in a simplistic way the studies that conclude that the greater the incidence of subordinate clauses the greater the maturity of the writer. It is much more to do with the ability to make explicit the interrelationships between propositions, phenomena or events; and to be able to express these links in the linguistic surface of the text. As I noted in chapter 1 such links in speech often remain implicit. Development in writing, in this sense, is not to be seen as a greater use *per se* of clause types but rather as the ability to use appropriate types of clauses to make explicit the relationships between events or propositions.

Other features that occur in this broad category are the use of nominalizations – *its normal flight* instead of *it normally flies* – and more elaborate noun phrases, particularly in subject position. Perera (1984) offers a comprehensive description of this aspect of writing development. However, as she observes, it is important to stress that little but harm will be achieved by teaching such constructions explicitly as was done in the practice of sentence-combining exercises. Development needs to be related to the overall understanding of the processes of creating texts that convey meaning with clarity and economy.

The second aspect, then, of the move from speech-like uses of language entails a growing appreciation and knowledge of those text types that are specific to the written mode. Some of these were described in chapter 2 and I will not repeat what was written there. However, it is worth emphasizing that the development of pupils' knowledge and understanding of text types is an important aspect of the teaching of writing. Procedures for effecting this will be discussed later.

4.4.3 The independent writer

The third major aspect of development can be described as an increasing independence and self-reliance as a writer. Earlier in this chapter I described in detail techniques that are designed to help young writers. All these in varied ways give supports that reduce the total load on the pupil when he or she is beginning to write. It follows that development can, in part, be seen in the ability of a writer eventually to be able to operate successfully without these carefully structured supports. Independence, however, is always relative and may be seen also in the ability to know where to go to get the necessary help. A teacher of ESL pupils complained to me recently that her 15-year-olds still needed to use their dictionaries when writing – and that was after a full five years of learning to write in English. I observed to her that I still needed to use a dictionary after nearly forty years of writing English as a native speaker!

4.5 Reading and writing

I suggested earlier in this chapter that young writers will be helped in their development by the planned provision of a range of texts which can become the focus for reading and reflective discussion, and can develop pupils' understanding of the range and nature of text types. This illustrates a general point about writing: writing cannot be seen in isolation from other modes of language use – it requires attention to reading and to talking as two of the means by which it can be fostered. In this sense, it is strange to hear people talk about the 'writing classroom' as if writing could somehow be isolated from other aspects of language or indeed from learning as a whole. (It may be, however, that this use of the term should not be taken too literally.)

Reading and the consideration of written texts should form an important part of the teaching of writing. Although it is helpful if pupils read voluntarily a wide range of texts, we should not take it for granted that this is likely even for a minority of pupils whether they be L1 or L2 learners. Nor should we assume that a cursory reading is always enough in itself to enable some transfer to writing to occur.

There are several levels at which reading feeds into writing. The most clear-cut is at the level of the overall structure of the text. It is commonly – and rightly – remarked that children can create texts, even in the early stages of writing, that show the hallmarks of narratives – story-markers such as *Once upon a time*, the use of events and the marking of a resolution by a tag such as *They all lived happily ever after* – and that this ability derives from the diet of stories heard, watched, shared and eventually read by themselves. With non-fiction there is not the same tradition of reading aloud or even much encouragement for children to read such texts for themselves. Yet, if we are to support pupils in the writing of an ever increasing range of texts, we need to give attention to ways in which we can develop awareness of the structures of such texts. I do not think it is a simple matter of providing more non-fiction books in the school and class libraries, though that is important; nor is it a matter of providing a single 'model' text as is common practice in ESL/EFL teaching. The relationship between reading and writing is more complex. There is a parallel with the relationship between reading and spelling that will help to make my point clear. A fluent reader is not necessarily a good speller, despite popular opinion. A good speller is likely to be someone who not only reads widely but is interested in words and thinks about them. People who habitually do crossword puzzles are likely to be good spellers, even if that leaves little time for wider reading. Fluent readers, on the other hand, may sometimes be relatively poor spellers because they read quickly and do not at the same time register the shape and patterns of words. In the same way, it is from the growing awareness of the structures of texts that pupils will derive the internalized models that they need as they develop as writers. This cannot be achieved on a one-to-one basis, as follows:

Read a recipe → Produce a recipe

The relationship is more like that shown in the figure opposite. A growing awareness of text types can also be enhanced by the use of strategies that are often seen as related only to reading. An example is the use of 'scrambled' texts in which the original order of the paragraphs has been changed. Pupils have to reorder the paragraphs in order to create a coherent text. This kind of work is

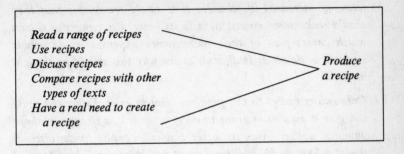

best done by groups of pupils because the discussions about overall **coherence** and how it is related at a more localized level to the links between sentences and paragraphs are the essence of the developing awareness. Getting the right answer is not, in itself, important. The following activity illustrates the point.

ACTIVITY

The following paragraphs constitute the complete text of a letter to a newspaper. The order in which the paragraphs are presented is random. Decide on the most appropriate and coherent order. Note your reasons and the means whereby the paragraphs are linked to each other and by which the text achieves coherence as a whole.

4d

1 *Britain has the most generous system of State support for students, yet access to higher education lags behind that of many of our competitors.*

2 *In so far as higher education provides for the country's future prosperity, it is not clear why the entire cost of it should fall upon the State. After all, highly-qualified graduates, especially in science and technology, generally stand to gain from higher salaries.*

3 *As students are the principal beneficiaries of higher education in*

terms of increased life-chances it is surely reasonable that they should make some contribution to its costs. Repayment of a loan which covers part of their maintenance expenses would enable students to do so. It is difficult to see why this should be thought immoral.

4 *Only two remedies to this problem seem to exist. Either the State can give a maximum grant to every student – a strange, perhaps immoral, option, given the other claims on public funds; alternatively, a loan as an additional source of income can be offered. I prefer the latter option.*

5 *If resources saved through a system of loans were used to boost access, that would be both wise and 'morally justified'.*

6 *As an enthusiast for 'top-up' loans, I would make the following points in response to your correspondent of November 16th, who asks whether they can be morally justified.*

7 *The current system of student support itself has many flaws. In particular, 35 per cent of parents do not make the financial contribution which is expected of them. As a result, many students do experience hardship.*

The order of the original letter is: 6, 3, 2, 7, 4, 1, 5.

The first stage in determining an appropriate order is to select the opening paragraph. Either 1 or 6 appear to be possible. Paragraph 1 makes a general statement of the sort that often, at the beginning of a text, signals the topic of the whole text – the thesis. However, 6 is the more likely choice because it contains a reason for the whole text (*make the following points in response*) and a declaration of point of view (*as an enthusiast for 'top-up' loans*). The phrase *the following points* also serves to signal the structure of the text that follows – it is a series of points in response to a previous letter which raised the question of the morality of 'top-up' loans. Once the decision is made to place 6 in initial position in preference to 1, the function of 1 can be seen as a general summarizing one. This paragraph is linked to 5 (many writers would not, in fact, have divided these into two separate paragraphs and we can only presume that the writer did so to provide an emphatic conclusion). Paragraph 5 serves as a link back to the opening question of moral justification.

The order of the rest of the text is composed of two groups each of two paragraphs. Paragraphs 7 and 4 form the most obvious group. Paragraph 7 sets up a problem signalled by *many students do experience hardship*. The possible solutions to this problem of hardship are contained in 4, signalled by *two remedies*; and the writer opts for his preferred choice *I prefer the latter option*. Paragraphs 3 and 2 stand in a general-to-particular relationship, signalled by the phrases *increased life-chances* and *higher salaries* which is a specific aspect of the increased life-chances. In determining the order of these two groups – 3 and 2, 7 and 4 – it is the progression of the argument and the move from general to particular that suggests 3/2 should precede 7/4.

Here is the original text in full:

4e

As an enthusiast for 'top-up' loans, I would make the following points in response to your correspondent of November 16th, who asks whether they can be morally justified.

As students are the principal beneficiaries of higher education in terms of increased life-chances it is surely reasonable that they should make some contribution to its costs. Repayment of a loan which covers part of their maintenance expenses would enable students to do so. It is difficult to see why this should be thought immoral.

In so far as higher education provides for the country's future prosperity, it is not clear why the entire cost of it should fall upon the State. After all, highly-qualified graduates, especially in science and technology, generally stand to gain from higher salaries.

The current system of student support itself has many flaws. In particular, 35 per cent of parents do not make the financial contribution which is expected of them. As a result, many students do experience hardship.

Only two remedies to this problem seem to exist. Either the State can give a maximum grant to every student – a strange, perhaps immoral, option, given the other claims on public funds; alternatively, a loan as an additional source of income can be offered. I prefer the latter option.

Britain has the most generous system of State support for students, yet access to higher education lags behind that of many of our competitors.

If resources saved through a system of loans were used to boost access, that would be both wise and 'morally justified'.

So far we have been considering the overall structure of texts with some reference to more local features such as **cohesive ties**. This emphasis is not random but reflects a belief that it is important to concentrate first and foremost on the text as a whole rather than individual paragraphs or sentences. Approaches to writing that emphasize notional paragraph structures and that concentrate on sentence-by-sentence text building without relating these to the text as a whole will not give the writer a sense that he or she is creating texts that are in any genuine sense meaningful. Attention to sentence, clause, phrase and word levels of language will be helpful only if they are seen as contributing to the total meaning of the text.

4.6   Spelling

I suggested earlier that good spellers are not necessarily fluent readers, though they may be, but are almost invariably people who have an interest in words and perceive both the shapes and patterns of words. They will also have good visual memories and be disposed to get things right. Knowing this provides us with a basis for a positive strategy for teaching spelling – one that is based on helping pupils to acquire and extend their visual perception of words. The most popular technique for achieving this is to give pupils words they need using what is called the 'look-cover-write-check' strategy. These are the stages:

1. Write the word on a piece of paper – an A4 sheet divided into four is ideal.
2. The pupil looks at the word as you say it in a normal speaking voice – that is, with no distortion of the pronunciation.
3. The pupil says the word while still looking at it.
4. The paper is covered or turned face down.
5 The pupil writes the word from memory.
6. The pupil checks to see if the spelling is correct. If it is, it can be entered into the pupil's word-book. If not, the error should be discussed and stages 2 to 6 repeated.

Although this takes a little longer than simply writing the word in the pupil's word-book or sounding it out, it has been found by teachers to be worth the extra time because more often than not it leads to the word being committed to a pupil's long-term memory. If a word is just written in a word-book it is unlikely that it will be committed to memory; learning will not have taken place but rather a mechanical act of copying. If a word is sounded out, a pupil is having to make the transition from aural symbols to visual symbols which is potentially confusing, particularly in a language like English which does not have a regular correspondence between sounds and symbols.

It follows that the second basis for teaching spelling must take into account the writing system of English. Popular belief is that English is a difficult language because it operates on a sound-symbol correspondence but does not do it with any reliability. Although it is difficult to learn to spell in English, more so for native speakers who are inclined to operate on a simple sound-symbol correspondence, the fact is that English like several other languages does not work simply on a sound-symbol relationship. The form of words is also an important factor. Technically, this means that the English writing system is organized on a **morpho-phonemic** basis – sound and form together relate to meaning. Spelling strategies should be designed to help pupils appreciate the structures and patterns of words.

ACTIVITY

Read the following groups of words aloud and consider the relative importance of form over sound in identifying relationships:

4f

ease	*globe*	*do*
easy	*global*	*does*
disease	*globule*	*don't*
uneasy		
easiness		
remedy	*soft*	
remedial	*soften*	*photograph*
remediation	*softly*	*photography*
		photographic
finite	*sign*	
infinite	*signature*	
infinity	*resignation*	
definite	*signal*	
definitely	*assignment*	
definitive	*design*	
infinitive		

In each group the visual pattern of the words is the more reliable guide to the family likeness. Sometimes the sound is altered because the stress falls on a different syllable when an **affix** is added – for example *REmedy* but *reMEdial*. In the case of *soft* and *soften* the change in sound is extreme and reliance on sounding out will inevitably lead to error. Each group also illustrates the great importance in English morphology of affixes. Affixes are divided into two classes – **prefixes** that are added at the front of the root word and **suffixes** that are added after the root word, as in: *EASE*; *DIS + EASE* (prefix *DIS + ease*); *EASY* (*ease* + suffix *Y*); *EASINESS* (*ease* + suffixes *I* and *NESS*). It may seem odd that *easy* has a terminal *+ y* while *easiness* has *+ i* before the final suffix. This is because native English words (as opposed to **loan words** such as *taxi* and *ski*) cannot end in *+ i*: to avoid this happening final *+ i* becomes *+ y*.

It is important to note that emphasizing the form of words, particularly affixes, is not the same thing as emphasizing the syllabic structure of words. Identifying syllables helps us to see how word stress operates in English; it can sometimes aid pronunciation but, emphatically, it does not assist in any way with spelling. For example, *unusually* has five syllables but identifying these does not help with spelling the word. The word has three parts which technically are called **morphemes**, as follows: prefix *un*, root *usual*, suffix *ly*. Each of these parts contributes to the meaning of the word – apart from the meaning of the root, *un* indicates + negative and *ly* is an adverbial marker. In contrast, syllables carry no grammatical significance.

One last point can be illustrated through the *finite* group. Among the most common errors I have encountered – not only in pupils' writing but in that of students in higher education – is **definate*. This error occurs because people are operating on a sound-symbol basis. Once they perceive the family relationship between *finite*, *infinite* and *definite* they are usually able to correct their error which is, in fact, based on a misconception about spelling.

So far I have suggested that strategies for teaching spelling should put an emphasis on building up a visual memory of words and an understanding of the significance of the form of words. The last point to make is that pupils will be helped to develop positive attitudes if spelling is set firmly in perspective. It is important to establish that we do not write to spell but that we need to be able to spell to assist the fluency and communicative force of our writing. Spelling is a means to an end; it should never become an end in itself.

4.7 Punctuation

Halliday (1989) provides a fascinating account of the development of punctuation as a feature of writing systems. He points out that Greek was originally written without word boundaries and without any punctuation. A written text was, therefore, a solid block of symbols. In Greek the direction alternated from left to right and right to left. Developments over time have lead to the system of punctuation in English as we now know it. Halliday lists the following features in their order of occurrence:

1. Line direction
2. Spaces between words
3. The full stop to mark sentence boundaries
4. Symbols to distinguish between lower case and capital letter uses
5. Special symbols such as hyphens, brackets and apostrophes to mark linkages, interpolations and omissions
6. Commas, colons, semicolons and dashes
7. Quotation marks (single and double inverted commas), question marks and exclamation marks

(Halliday 1989: 33)

Interestingly, the question mark derives from the Latin *quaestio* and the exclamation mark from the Latin exclamatory cry *io* written thus ! and these were introduced in medieval times to indicate the status of a sentence.

Punctuation is fundamentally a means of marking boundaries and relationships between the grammatical units of written texts.

The most clear-cut uses of punctuation are those that mark the boundaries of the most obvious grammatical units. They are also the most fixed and unvarying in usage. As Carter (1992) points out in an unpublished manuscript (on which I have drawn extensively in this brief account of the teaching of punctuation), punctuation can be usefully divided into rules and conventions. The rules generally mark the obvious grammatical boundaries. In written text, as I have already stressed, the sentence is the fundamental unit; it is also a grammatical unit. Accordingly, we find that the use of a full stop to mark a sentence boundary is an almost unvarying rule (but see below for exceptions). The use of a question mark to denote the boundary of an interrogative sentence is also a rule. However, the use of the exclamation mark for expressive purposes is a convention that is very much a matter of personal preference.

It may be useful to think of the relationship between punctuation and meaning as operating on two parallel continua – one that moves from rules to conventions, the other from marking relationships that are grammatically defined to those that are expressive, as follows:

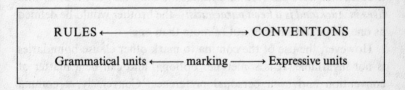

If we apply these continua to examples, we can see that the use of the full stop is a clear instance of a punctuation rule that marks a grammatical boundary. In the following sentence, however, the grammatical units are not altered in any way by a change in punctuation but the expressive meaning is: *Her first recital in Moscow was a triumph.* In this version the intended reading is that this refers to the artist's Moscow debut. If it is punctuated like this

– *Her first recital, in Moscow, was a triumph* – the intended meaning is that the artist's debut recital was a triumph and it was, incidentally, in Moscow. This is an example of a punctuation convention which marks the expressive meaning of the text, not a grammatical boundary.

The comma, in fact, is the most difficult of all the punctuation marks to use because it occurs sometimes at the left-hand end of the two continua but just as often at the right-hand end. It marks expressive uses, and in such cases its use is a matter of convention, but there are also uses that are rule-bound. The most common of the rules governing the use of the comma is in lists where items in a series are separated by a comma unless linked by a co-ordinating conjunction, as in: *For lunch that day we had congee, ducks' webs, steamed fish-balls, deep-fried beancurd and stir-fried green vegetables.*

Another rule governing the use of the comma is for marking off disjuncts such as *however, in fact* and *nevertheless.* It is also used for marking relative clauses that are non-defining (that is, giving additional information that is only incidental). An example of this is *My brother, who lives in Auckland, is a keen parachutist* where the important information is that the brother is a parachutist. If the sentence were punctuated without the commas – *My brother who lives in Auckland is a keen parachutist* – the brother would be defined as one particular brother out of more than one.

However, the use of the comma to mark other clause boundaries is not invariable. It is sometimes optional and can be a matter of convention and even personal preference. Conversely, a comma cannot mark off the clause boundary when the clause is a noun clause in subject position in a sentence, as in: *That using censorship in an attempt to prevent open discussion of ideas is a counter-productive measure has yet again been proven by the popularity of the covertly distributed, but previously banned materials.*

Faced by what appear to be complex and sometimes arbitrary rules and conventions, teachers need to have a set of priorities for helping students with punctuation. Incidentally, it is important that teachers of experienced writers in a mother tongue who are learning to write English as their L2 should not assume that the punctuation systems will be the same. As a set of priorities I would suggest one that closely follows the list given by Halliday (1989) for the development of punctuation historically. The first two items – line direction and spaces between words – will be of concern only with beginning writers of English, both L1 and L2 learners. The first main emphasis needs to be on the use of the full stop to mark sentence boundaries. Here we need to bear in mind that the fundamental need is for pupils to perceive what are sentence units rather than to impose on them rules that they cannot apply without that prior understanding. Question marks should also be introduced soon after – with the same proviso – that pupils need to be aware of the communicative nature of a question before any insistence is made on the use of the question mark in writing.

Since story writing is a favoured activity in the early stages of writing, it may well be appropriate to introduce speech marks when it is apparent that pupils are attempting to use dialogue in their stories. Here again, it is important that pupils are helped first to distinguish speech from the narrative before the rules for punctuating direct speech are introduced. A simple and effective way of doing this is to start by asking pupils to circle the speech in their stories. Once the speech is correctly identified the punctuation marks can be substituted for the circles.

The more sophisticated punctuation marks – colons, semicolons and dashes – are not vital to effective writing but can be useful as writers increasingly need to express more subtle and complex relationships. The semicolon can, for instance, be used in place of a full stop to indicate a particularly strong relationship between two units that are nevertheless grammatically defined as sentences, as in: *She was a popular teacher; she always had time for all her pupils*.

The colon is useful as a device for introducing lists or examples. As Halliday (1989) points out, it is typically used cataphorically (that is, it refers forwards in the text).

There remains the most common problem in English punctuation, the use of the apostrophe. In this the boundary between spelling and punctuation becomes contentious but the problem has to be solved by the teacher in a practical way. To look at the use of the apostrophe and at teaching approaches the following activity will be helpful.

ACTIVITY

Look at the following groups of words. Determine the punctuation rule governing the words in the list. Then decide on a teaching order for the groups.

4g

A	his	B	his	C	I'm
	her		hers		you're
	its		ours		she's
	our		yours		he's
	your		theirs		it's
	their				we're
	whose				they're
					who's

D	Jake's thing	E	Dickens' novels
	Rosie's walk		Dickens's novels
	Friday's child		Keats' letters
	The King's Head		Keats's letters

F	it's	G	others' lives
	there's		commentators' jargon
			authors' rights
			investors' dreams
			developers' profits

The apostrophe is used principally to indicate possession. This is shown in groups D and E. Group D is the most straightforward. In this the apostrophe $+ s$ is used; it is a survival from the Old English genitive ending -*es* which marked possession. And it is in this historical sense that this use of the apostrophe is arguably more a matter of spelling than of punctuation. Group G illustrates the formation of the plural possessive form with -*s'*. The last group that indicates possession through the use of the apostrophe is E. This is a relatively uncommon usage and is a matter of preference – both the -*s'* and the -*s's* forms are accepted, even if individuals sometimes espouse one or the other with pedantic and wrong-headed fanaticism!

The other use of the apostrophe is to mark contracted forms. We find this in groups C and F. The forms *its* and *it's* are commonly confused. It seems to me that it is much more helpful to show students groups of words that establish a likeness through which rules of usage can be perceived rather than to present forms that can cause confusion when placed side-by-side as a contrast. Thus, *it's* as a contracted form is best grouped as in groups C and F. The possessive form, *its*, is better understood and remembered through its similarity with the other possessive and reflexive pronouns, as in groups A and B.

Punctuation, taken as a whole, needs to be related to the meaning of a stretch of written language. There are some simple rules that can be taught, as seen in the last activity. However, these apart, a general guiding principle for classroom practice is that punctuation is best discussed on a one-to-one basis. This means that it can be related to a particular text and to the writer's intended meaning. It is, incidentally, no use trying to equate punctuation with the pauses that occur in speech. The pauses in speech do not consistently follow either grammatical or meaning units; they are much more random, often indicating that the speaker is hesitating over the choice of a word. Reading a written text aloud at a draft stage, however, can be a useful strategy through which a writer can clarify the intended meaning and thus perceive the way in which punctuation can help to achieve this. Halliday (1989) explores this issue thoroughly as part of a wide-ranging discussion of the differences and similarities between speech and writing.

SUMMARY

- Writing in the classroom must have a clearly perceived and explicitly formulated purpose.
- Young writers need support to help them cope with the many demands in the early stages of writing development.
- Reading and writing should be closely integrated in the language classroom and in the teaching of content areas across the curriculum.
- Spelling and punctuation are both important aspects of writing. They need to be related to the appropriate stage of the process of writing and to be taught positively in the context of how each contributes to the meaning of a text.

5   Assessing and reading texts

5.1   Perspectives on assessing writing

At the present time there is a great emphasis on accountability in education. The reasons for this are many and complex; they have been and are still being debated in many countries. Assessment is usually seen as the main instrument by which success in education can be measured – not just the success of the individual student but the success of the system itself. Assessment then becomes closely linked to accountability. In the present context I cannot enter into this debate at length but will outline a few points in order to place the assessment of writing in a wider perspective.

Accountability in education has become a dominant political issue in many societies because the cost of education is always a significant part of a country's overall expenditure. The cost can, of course, legitimately be seen as an investment for the future of the society, particularly in a world in which information-based technologies are of crucial importance to economic growth. These require adaptable and skilled people; there is less and less scope for the uneducated and unskilled in the present world even compared to thirty years ago. Governments naturally look to education systems to provide ever higher numbers of well-educated students to fulfil anticipated roles in their developing societies.

This requires an investment in education and it is but a simple step to apply the processes of the market place and insist on a visible return on this investment and a measure of control over the quality of the enterprise – hence the demand for accountability. The most visible measure of accountability is in the assessment of pupils' progress, typically through written examinations, tests or course work. Whether this is intrinsically desirable or not is open to question – but not a question that can be discussed here. What is important is that teachers should be quite clear about what they are doing when assessing writing.

It is usual to differentiate between formative and summative assessment. Summative assessment provides a basis for determining progress at a given stage such as the end of primary or compulsory schooling. It usually takes the form of tests or examinations and through it an individual's achievement is assessed comparatively against the achievements of other students, ranked in relation to norms of achievement – hence, the term norm-referenced assessment.

Formative assessment takes place over a period of time through which an individual's progress is observed and recorded by a variety of means. The main purpose is to provide information for the pupil, the teacher and others about the individual's learning – what is well understood and what is not. It is, therefore, primarily diagnostic and an aid to the development of learning by the pupil and to the facilitating of that learning by the teacher.

The emphasis on making the most of each pupil's abilities – an aspect of accountability – requires constant attention to, and checks on, individual progress. In relation to writing, this means that teachers need to be able to do more than to assign a generalized grade (A, B, C or Good, Average and so on) to a piece of writing; they also need to be able to read texts both as drafts and as finished products with as much insight as possible. The importance of being able to read pupils' writing effectively is underlined by another development in asssessment. Norm-referenced assessment, which is characteristic of end-of-stage assessment, is now gradually being replaced by criterion-referenced assessment. Instead of pupils' achievements being set against that of all other pupils in a national or regional year group and ranked accordingly, a pupil's achievement is measured against sets of criteria. The National Curriculum in England and Wales operates on this principle. The Target and

Target-Related Assessment initiative in Hong Kong will also function in a similar way.

Examples of some of the criteria for the assessment of writing in the National Curriculum for English in the UK are:

- at level 3 (out of 10 levels in all): write more complex stories with detail beyond simple events and with a defined ending.
- at level 4: discuss the organization of their own writing; revise and redraft the writing as appropriate, independently, in the light of that discussion.
- at level 7: write in a wider variety of forms, with commitment and a clear sense of purpose and awareness of audience, demonstrating an ability to anticipate the reader's response.

(DES, 1990)

These are just three examples; each level for writing contains four or five statements of attainment. In total there are forty statements for writing – excluding separate statements for spelling, handwriting and presentation, which is a combination of the two in the later stages of development. It will be immediately apparent that each statement requires interpretation, and to make sound interpretations requires careful and perceptive readings of pupils' texts – just as, one hopes, the formulation of the criteria has been based on a sound understanding of the development of pupils' writing abilities.

This, then, is the context in which the rest of the section is placed. It is a recognition of the need to assist teachers and teachers in training to make careful and perceptive readings of pupils' texts.

5.2 Readings of texts

The sample readings that follow (on pages 101–3) are selective in the sense that only certain issues are dealt with in relation to each text or group of texts. An ideal procedure would be to read each text and then discuss it with a colleague or group of colleagues before looking at the commentaries. I have not placed much emphasis on the contexts from which the writing arose, preferring to concentrate on the texts themselves. Teachers are usually sensitive to the contexts of writing and to pupils' individual needs; what is not so common is to find that they have been equipped through their training to 'read' children's writing at the levels of grammatical structure and text organization and to see how these both contribute to the total meaning of a text.

Three narratives (5a, 5b, 5c)

William's text (5a) is interesting from a developmental point of view. For a 6-year-old he shows the beginnings of an understanding of narrative structure. This can be seen in the use of the initial story-marker *Once upon a time.* The circumstances are also clearly set out. Where the story needs development is in the structuring of events and the expression of cause and effect. The reason why the bee could not eat honey was that there were no flowers. There were no flowers because it was winter. The ordering of the elements does create some ambiguity but this should not be regarded simply as a matter of sequencing. The underlying reason for the ambiguity is the failure to relate cause and effect. It is this that should be the focus for discussion with the writer.

This story also raises the issue of the relationship between pictures and stories. It is common in early years practice to find that children are encouraged to draw a picture before writing their stories. While this can be a useful strategy for motivating writing, there is an inherent danger that the story will become tied to the picture in a way that can be harmful. William avoids this potential problem most successfully. His text stands in its own right and does not need the picture to fulfil the meaning. He introduces the bee as *a bee* and the garden as *someone's garden.* If the text were a gloss on the picture we would expect to find *the bee is living in the garden* and the continued use of the present rather than the past tense. Many early reading scheme books present a similarly false model of language use to children. It is something that teachers need to be alert to.

Melanie's story (5b) is interesting from the point of view of structure. The elements of the setting are presented without any elaboration. Significantly, there is no mention of any motivating reason for the midnight walk. This omission weakens the impact of the

5a

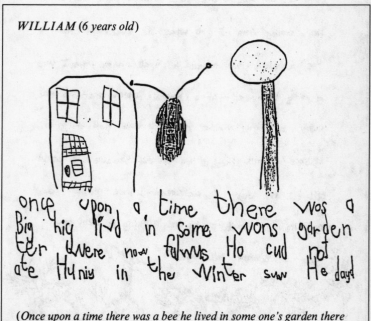

WILLIAM (6 years old)

once upon a time there was a
Big hig livd in some wons garden
ter were now flwws Ho cud not
ate Huniy in the Winter suw He dayd

(*Once upon a time there was a bee he lived in some one's garden there were no flowers he could not eat honey in the winter so he died*)

(Author's data)

5b

MELANIE (7 years old)

A walk in a creepy wood

One dark night at midnight I went for a walk
I saw a wood . It was scarey . I went in it . I
heard something . I looked up It was something but I
could not see what it was so I followed where the sound
was coming from . I got where the noise came from . it
was a witch . She made a spell on me . Then I was
a frog because of that horrible witch . The witch went
away . I heard another noise it was something in
a tree . I knew that it was an owl because I could
tell . I ran away . I screamed . I went home . told
my mum all about it . In the morning I went back
again . It. started all again.

(Author's data)

5c

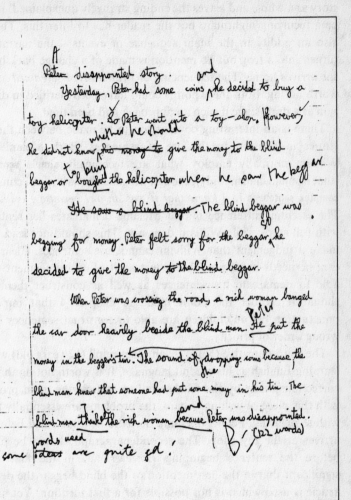

A

~~Peter~~ disappointed story.

Yesterday, Peter had some coins ʌand he decided to buy a toy helicopter. So Peter went into a toy–shop. However, he did not know ~~this money to~~ ʌwhether he should give the money to the blind beggar or <u>to buy</u> ~~bought~~ the helicopter when he saw the beggar

~~He saw a blind beggar.~~ The blind beggar was begging for money. Peter felt sorry for the beggar, ʌso he decided to give the money to the blind beggar.

When Peter was crossing the road, a rich woman banged the car door heavily beside the blind man. ʌPeter He put the money in the beggar's tin. The sound of dropping coins because the blind man knew that someone had put some money in his tin. The blind man thanked the rich woman ʌand because Peter was disappointed.

some ~~ideas~~ <u>words used</u> are quite gd.   B (122 words)

(Author's data)

story as a whole and leaves the ending strangely unexplained. It may be a recurring nightmare but the reader has to infer this. There is also an oddity in the main sequence of events – the narrator is turned into a frog but no mention is made of a change back before she arrives home. The sequencing of *I ran away. I screamed.* is also worth noting. Both these points could have been clarified in discussion at a draft stage if such an approach had been used.

There is an interesting comparison to be made between the two stories in relation to the use of sentences. Both Melanie and William normally employ what are technically **simple sentences** (that is, main clauses only), though Melanie shows she can construct **complex sentences** in *I knew that it was an owl because I could tell.* The essential difference is that Melanie demarcates her sentences with full stops while William does not. This should not lead us to make a judgement that William cannot use sentences. Clearly he can; he needs in all probability just a bit of encouragement to be able to demarcate his sentences as well as construct them. We should remember the point made in chapter 4 that imposing punctuation before children are able to construct sentences is the wrong order of priority.

The third narrative (5c) is by an older pupil (12 years old) who is learning English as his second language. It is worth noting that the corrections made by the teacher fail to address the main problem with this piece of writing. Again, the problems are essentially to do with sequencing. Peter's dilemma needs to be established before he arrives at the toy shop. The second paragraph should be placed before the sentence beginning *However, ...* in the first. It is significant that in the first mention of the blind beggar the definite article is used which is not possible for a first mention. Yet, in the second paragraph, the mention (crossed out by the teacher) uses the indefinite article – correctly for a first mention.

It is, in fact, the problem with sequencing rather than with any of the surface mistakes noted by the teacher that makes the story in its present state unsatisfactory. Significantly, the writer had to write out a corrected version incorporating the teacher's changes but, because there was no drafting or discussion, the sequencing issue was not addressed. This illustrates vividly the dangers of becoming absorbed in the grammar and vocabulary of a text and not looking at the overall organization. It shows also that L2 writers need help with structure more than they do with grammar and vocabulary, just as L1 writers do. Without the attention to overall structure, the attention to grammar and vocabulary can become meaningless.

Pigeon texts (5d, 5e)

These two texts are considered in some detail since they enable a useful comparison to be made between a personal account and an informative report. This material was originally part of the LINC training materials.

5d

THE DEAD PIGEON

To day at afternoon play just when we was comeing back in to school Mrs B found a pidgin on the floor next to the Haygreen Lane side Some children had gone in but I was ther when Gary Destains said hay up thers a pidgin on floor. We all rusht up but Mrs B showted "stop come back and let me look whats apend to it poor thing." I just thout it was resting a bit but Dobbie said its ded it was when Mrs B picket it up its kneck just flopped over poor thing I said to Dobbie. She lifted it up with its wings and they were like big lovely grey fans. I didn't know wings were so lovely and big with so meny fethers espeshily When we had gon in we was just sittind in are class and telling Mrs Sandison and the others about it when Mrs B came and held it up with its lovly grey wings I was sorry for it poor thing and Mrs Sandison was sad and we all was.

(Lesley, Year 5)

5e

THE WOOD PIGEON

The wood pigeon has a pees of red on its beak at the top and yellow at the end. When you look closely at it it isnt only grey and white it has litish green and purple just near the neck part. It has right little feathers on it head not long ones like the wings. Its head is very soft. The wood pigeon is a bird of the woods but since the spread of agriculture it has taken to feeding on cultivated land It is a familiar bird in parks and gardens. It is quite tame in the parks. Its normal flight is fast and strong with quick regular wingbeats and occasional glides on the ground it struts. It roosts in trees and its voice can be heard at all times of the year but mainly in March and April. It is often said to coo. Cereal grains are most important food. When we were in London my dad got a bag of seeds for me and Joanne and the pigens came right up to us. Joanne was scared. My dads friend Jim rases pigeons but not wood I don't think.

(*Martin, Year 5*)

(*both 10 years old*)

(Author's data)

These texts were written by two children in the same class, in response to the incident graphically described in Lesley's piece. She writes a personal narrative while Martin offers an information report. Martin spent some time on his report, incorporating some research into the topic, while Lesley wrote her piece quickly and without revisions. To consider the two texts together provides useful contrasts:

LESLEY	MARTIN
Personal narrative	Information report
	non-narrative/
	non-chronological
specific incident	generalized information
past tense	present tense

At an organizational level the contrast that is most obvious is between the chronology that structures Lesley's piece and the non-chronological basis of Martin's. Lesley uses the actual occurrence of events to provide the ordering of the sentences in the text. However, it is not quite as simple as that. The order of events reported in the first sentences is in actuality:

1. Some children go into school after play
2. Others including Lesley follow behind
3. Gary finds a pigeon on the floor
4. The group of children rush to see it
5. Mrs B calls for them to stop

Lesley, in fact, manipulates this sequence in a sophisticated way. She puts the focus of the first main clause on Mrs B finding the pigeon (*Mrs B found a pidgin* . . .). In the second sentence (*Some children had gone in but I was ther*) she builds up a comparison which provides a focus for her own participation (*I was ther*), using the past (*had gone*) to contrast with (*was*). The event that might appear most significant, the finding of the pigeon, is then recounted in the subordinated adverbial time clause, *when Gary Destains said* . . . This again throws prominence onto her own participation, consistent with the personal nature of her account.

In the third sentence Mrs B, as it were, takes control of the situation. This provides the answer to the apparent contradiction between the first sentence (*Mrs B found a pidgin*) and the second, which provides the information that Gary was the first to notice the pigeon. Lesley, in fact, is concerned primarily with her own involvement in the incident and secondarily with her reactions to it. She also sees Mrs B as the central figure in the finding of the pigeon because she was presumably the teacher on duty.

It is generally to be expected that a chronological or time-related sequence of events will contain time expressions. Apart from the circumstance elements just noted in the first sentence, Lesley uses several adverbial time clauses in her text which emphasize its time-related nature: *just when we was comeing back in to school/when Gary Destains said/when Mrs B picket it up/when we had gon in/when Mrs B came.*

SENTENCES AND PUNCTUATION

It is also noteworthy that the grammatical structure of clauses and sentences is well handled, though the absence of punctuation does, at times, hinder comprehension. For instance, the fifth sentence, as punctuated in the text, might be read as *It was when Mrs B . . .*, since this is a construction that might be anticipated in the light of the number of adverbial clauses and the comparative absence of simple sentences. Lesley, however, shows a fitting dramatic control in her writing as can be seen in this edited version of the passage: *I just thought it was resting a bit but Dobbie said, 'It's dead.' It was. When Mrs B picked it it up, its neck just flopped over. 'Poor thing,' I said to Dobbie.*

A similar instance of possible ambiguity is to be found in part of Martin's text: *Its normal flight is fast and strong with quick regular wing beats and occasional glides on the ground it struts.* Here, the lack of punctuation after *glides* could be confusing.

CHOICE OF VOCABULARY IN THE TWO TEXTS

Lesley's account is highly personal and anecdotal. The particularity of place and persons that is so central to her text shows in the speech and more so in the regional dialect forms which are, of course, perfectly legitimate in speech situations. Lesley, however, does on a few occasions use dialect forms that are not appropriate in the main narrative. There are three instances of *we was* where the Standard English form appropriate to writing is *we were*.

Martin, on the other hand, is writing a more formal information report in which there is no place for dialogue and in which the regional dialect in *It has right little feathers on it head* is inappropriate.

CIRCUMSTANCES

It is also interesting to note the emphasis given to elements that describe the circumstances.

As well as participants and processes, sentences contain slots for circumstances, as follows:

S   participant
V   process
O   participant
C   further information about participant(s)
A   circumstances.

(see **sentence** in glossary for notation)

In Melanie's story, for instance, circumstances do not receive much emphasis, although the story's title is suggestive of eerie circumstances. Lesley, however, gives great prominence to circumstances. Apart from the main clause (*Mrs B found a pidgin*) all the other elements in the first sentence describe circumstances. This gives great particularity to the account and this is also evidenced in the number of personal pronouns and specific names in the text.

EXPRESSION OF FEELINGS

Lesley's reactions are recounted in three main ways. She uses a considerable number of words and phrases of an expressive nature – for example, *lovely and big*, *big lovely grey fans*. She also uses colloquial specifying words and phrases such as *just* (*thout*), (*resting*) *a bit*, (*so meny fethers*) *espeshily*. In the second part of the text, event and action processes give place to mental and relational processes – feelings replace doings. This, naturally enough, provides a resolution to the incident. Lesley leaves the reader with her reactions and those of her friends and teachers. Thus the structure as well as the grammatical choices serve to emphasize her personal involvement in the incident rather than the facts of the incident.

LESLEY'S WRITING COMPARED WITH MARTIN'S

This analysis provides a way of identifying the nature and extent of Lesley's achievement. It shows her confident control over the handling of time and tense, her conscious manipulation of sentence and clause structures to throw into prominence her own involvement in the incident, and the use of attitudinal expressions to record her reactions. The analysis also offers a guide to the typical linguistic features of a personal account or narrative which can be compared with Martin's information report.

Martin does not have a sequence of actual events which can provide a basis for the organization of his text. Instead, there are groupings of features:

— what its head looks like
— where it lives
— how it flies
— other habits and features.

Consistent with an information report, in subject position there are mentions of the wood pigeon or of specific features. This provides an immediate point of comparison with Lesley's text. The table opposite shows the subjects of the main clauses in each text.

The subjects in Lesley's text are persons; in Martin's the wood pigeon (referred to as a species marked linguistically by *the* initially) is almost the sole focus until the last few sentences, where the mould of the information report breaks down and a personal account follows – present tenses give way to the past, and persons occupy subject positions.

Other features of Martin's text that reveal a control over the type or genre he is attempting are:

— An effective use of a simple present tense – the simple present is a key language form which functions not so much to convey presentness as to support generic, general descriptions. The simple present gives us a modality of general truth and fact: *it roosts*; *it struts*.

LESLEY	MARTIN
Mrs B	*The wood pigeon*
Some children	*it . . . it*
but I	*It*
We all	*Its head*
but Mrs B	*The wood pigeon . . . it*
I	*It*
but Dobbie	*It*
It	*It*
its neck	*Its normal flight*
I	*it*
She	*It*
and they	*It*
I	*Cereal grains*
we	*my dad*
I	*and the pigeons*
and Mrs Sandison	*Joanne*
and we	*My dads friend Jim*

— Martin makes effective use of passives which serve to depersonalize the writing, to help impart a certain objective contour to what is stated: *It is often said to coo, its voice can be heard at all times of year*. Passives are highly appropriate to information report genres.

— Another feature which Martin handles well is modification. Examples of modifying words are: *mainly, normal, occasional*. They serve to modify what is said, putting appropriate qualifications and reservations on the statements.

— Finally, and surprisingly, Martin's text contains nominalizations. That is, instead of saying *It normally flies*, he writes *Its normal flight*; instead of saying *by beating its wings quickly* Martin writes *with quick wingbeats*. A nominalizing style is rare in spoken discourse (you find it more extensively in written texts) and Martin has effectively appropriated it for his information report. Nominalizations describe things with nouns rather than verbs. The whole process serves to remove agency and to depersonalize the text in ways appropriate to an impersonal reporting style.

It is, according to language development research, unusual for 10-year-olds to nominalize; and there is, therefore, a possibility that Martin has modelled these sentences on something he has read. This does not in any sense invalidate his achievement. If he has used models, however closely, the real point is that he has used them appropriately. It is also notable that Martin does not yet use such forms consistently. Development could be seen as achieving a greater consistency and also a more precise differentiation between genres; hence, there is a need for an eventual understanding that the personal anecdote interrupts the information report.

Smoking drafts (5f, 5g, 5h)

These drafts, and the final text, were written collaboratively by four 12-year-old pupils. This sequence illustrates well the usefulness of planning sheets and drafting as discussed in chapter 3. The teacher had asked the class to create a text that was intended to persuade; the choice of topic was left to the pupils. The planning sheet is used to provide a list of smoking-related topics that the pupils felt the need to research – the financial cost of smoking and the poisonous substances in cigarettes. The point about the number of deaths is not pursued – presumably because the pupils could not find the relevant information in the resources at their disposal. The draft shows an interesting combination of fully formulated and note-like writing. From the draft the pupils were able, using a word processor, to complete a final text in which they have reorganized the information to create a satisfactory, coherent and persuasive text. They establish the harmfulness of smoking first, then concentrate on the cost, ending on a note of inducement to stop smoking rather than continuing with the warnings of the damaging substances inhaled. Thus they employ a variety of persuasive strategies, balancing the scientific information with an appropriate appeal to common sense.

It is the process of drafting that has enabled them to make this appropriate structuring of the materials. It is much less likely that without the drafting process they would have been so successful in producing a coherent and fittingly persuasive text. The drafting also allows them to take material from their researches and to reshape it in ways that are suited to persuasive writing: *Tar is a brown sticky substance which is collected in the lungs of all smokers* in the draft becomes . . . *your lungs* . . . in the final text. The usual

5f

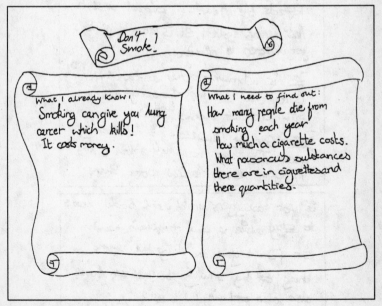

(Author's data)

5g

① Did you know that if you smoke you are consuming one of the most harmful poisons known to man. A pack of 20 cigarettes costs over £1.40, which means that just one cigarette costs approximatly 10p. And so, if you are daft enough to to smoke 50-55 cigarettes a day, you are spending appoximatly £2000 on them, every years, and for that, you could have an expensive holiday almost anywhere in the world!

② Nicoteen is a colourless chemical which Effects the heart + blood vessels And nervous system. It is also easy to get adicted to nicoteen

Tar is a brown sticky subtance which is collected In the lungs of all smokers. It causes lung cancer.

Carben Monoxide is a deadly gas which has no smell More C.M. in your blood, the less room there

is for oxygen, which the body needs to stay alive. If you complain about car fumes You are doing the same thing ot by smoking, because car fumes also also contain C.M. gas

(Author's data)

5h

```
NO TIME, NO MONEY, NO LIFE

DID YOU KNOW THAT IF YOU SMOKE YOU
ARE CONSUMING ONE OF THE MOST
HARMFUL POISONS KNOWN TO MAN.
THE THREE MOST HARMFUL THINGS IN
CIGARETTES ARE NICOTINE, TAR &
CARBON MONOXIDE.  NICOTINE IS A
COLOURLESS CHEMICAL WHICH AFFECTS
THE HEART, BLOOD VESSELS AND THE
NERVOUS SYSTEM.  TAR IS A BROWN
STICKY  SUBSTANCE WHICH WILL BE
COLLECTED IN YOUR LUNGS IF YOU
SMOKE.  CARBON MONOXIDE IS A DEADLY
GAS WITH NO SMELL. THE MORE OF THIS
YOU HAVE IN YOUR BLOOD, THE LESS
ROOM THERE IS FOR OXYGEN, WHICH THE
BODY NEEDS TO STAY ALIVE.
     A PACKET OF 20 CIGARETTES COSTS
OVER ONE POUND FORTY WHICH MEANS
THAT I CAN COST UP TO 1OP.  AND SO
IF YOU ARE DAFT ENOUGH TO SMOKE 55
PER DAY YOU ARE SPENDING ABOUT 2OOO
POUNDS A YEAR AND FROM THAT YOU
COULD HAVE AN EXPENSIVE HOLIDAY
ANYWHERE IN THE WORLD!!!!!!!!

        ELIZABETH
         JAMES
          ANDREW
           GILLIAN
```

(Author's data)

language features of persuasion are also evident – the use of questions, the use of the present tense and the second person address *you*.

In advertisements, cohesion (that is, the linkage between the sentences of a text) is characteristically achieved by the use of lexical chains – series of related vocabulary items. The features that additionally provide cohesion in narratives and expository writing such as the use of pronouns and conjunctions are much less commonly found. Lexical chains need, of course, to be related to and to support the overall argument of the text. This has been achieved remarkably well in the 'Smoking' drafts. The initial question mentions *harmful poisons*. These harmful poisons are then named and described – *nicotine, tar and carbon monoxide*. There is a related lexical chain that refers to the parts of the body affected – *heart, blood vessels, nervous system, lungs, blood.*

Litter

5i

> Litter problem is indeed a long lasting social problem. During the past few years, there are Keep Hong Kong Clean Campaigns and many other campaign activities which directly advise the citizens on not to litter.
>
> Nowadays, scientist have invented Ecolyte bio-degradable plastic bags. Moreover, education has been becoming an important means to persuade the new generation to keep everywhere clean.

Here is the text in full:

(*Litter problem is indeed a long-lasting social problem. During the past few years, there are Keep Hong Kong Clean Campaigns and many other activities which directly advise the citizens not to litter.*

Nowadays, scientist have invented Ecolyte bio-degradable plastic bags. Moreover, education has been becoming an important means to persuade the new generation to keep everywhere clean.

However, the result is disappointing after carrying out these money consuming activities. First of all, the campaigns are failed because teenagers like to rebel correct action. This characteristic is enough to make the campaigns all in vain.

On the other hand, the cost of Ecolyte bio-degradable plastic bags is much higher than common plastic bags. Furthermore, the plastic bag we use now have a large supply due to the immense demand from packaging industry. Thus, the bio-degradable plastic bag will only be effective if the production of non-biodegradable plastic bag is banned. In my point of view, government should utilize the mass media to tell citizens about the bad effects of littering which are greatly concerned to their surroundings. Then they would know the benefits of keeping a city clean and tidy.)

(*15-year-old, non-native speaker*)

(Author's data)

This text was written after the teacher had introduced the class to the topic of litter through a letter written to a local newspaper. The letter contained some difficult vocabulary items such as *intractable*, *eradicate* and *root out*. Preliminary discussion focused on these items but not on the word *litter* itself which does, in fact, present some problems of usage.

The text has a clear basic structure. The first two paragraphs set out the attempts being made to deal with the problem of litter. These are:

— campaigns and other activities to persuade people not to create litter

— invention of biodegradable plastic bags
— education as a means of influencing the young.

Each one of these possibilities is then evaluated in the rest of the text. The third point is evaluated first – educating the young about litter fails because of the rebellious nature of youth. Biodegradable plastic bags are also evaluated negatively because the costs of production are much higher than for conventional plastic bags, leading to the conclusion that economic factors will prevail unless a ban on the manufacture of the cheaper bags is imposed. The final paragraph evaluates the first point positively – that the only solution is for more and more effective propaganda.

This is a coherent and succinct structure. But while the argument has a sound progression, the use of conjunctions does not always support it. Conjunctions do not by themselves create the logical structure of a text; they signal or highlight it. In this piece the conjunctions do not always reinforce the underlying structure. It is as if the writer had been encouraged to use conjunctions as an exercise rather than to create a coherent argument and then see if the use of conjunctions could add to the clarity of the structure.

It is also notable that this is a piece of 'one-shot' writing. A process of drafting would have helped the writer to see how best to deploy conjunctions. It would also have provided an opportunity to deal with the instances of unidiomatic usage and the problems with tenses and with singular and plural forms (see Bunton and Green 1991 for a fuller discussion of these types of errors).

Reflex actions

5j

1 *Reflex actions are processes which occur within the body and are important to us in that they sometimes prevent us being seriously injured.*

2 *A reflex action is a response to a stimulus which occurs extremely quickly and does not require conscious thought.*

3 *This is because the impulses from the stimulus have only to travel to the spinal cord and not the brain.*

4 *Some reflex actions have to be learnt such as tying a shoe lace, chewing a pencil under stress and biting nails, but others come naturally from the moment we are born like digestion, breathing and jerking our big toe out of the bath water when we have forgotten to turn the cold tap on.*

5 *This latter fact forms the dividing line between the two categories of reflex action.*

6 *These are:*

   (a) conditioned which must be learnt and are our habits, personal to ourselves;

   (b) inborn which are instinctive and common to everyone.

7 *The following reflex pathway is the route along which impulses travel when we prick our hand on a sharp pin.*

8 *The stimulus is the pin which when pressed onto the hand, causes us to feel pain.*

9 *This pain is then converted into a nervous impulse which travels very rapidly along the sensory nerve towards the spinal cord.*

10 *It enters the spinal cord through the dorsal root of the spinal nerve from where it passes through the white matter and into the grey matter.*

11 *Here, the impulse jumps across the synapse between the sensory neurone and the connector neurone via the acetyl choline in the middle.*

12 *The same chemical is responsible for transferring the impulse to the neurone.*

13 *The motor neurone then leads the impulse out of the grey matter, the white matter and the ventral root of the spinal nerve.*

14 *The impulse finally arrives at the biceps by means of the motor end plate.*

15 *It causes the muscle to contract and hence the hand is pulled away from the pin.*

(16-year-old)

(Author's data)

The text has been laid out sentence by sentence for ease of reference. It was originally written with paragraph breaks after sentence 6 and after sentence 7 (S6 and S7).

The first thing to comment on is that the task itself is a strange one when viewed from a general rather than a school perspective. The instructions were to write an essay on the nature of reflex actions and then to describe the reflex pathway followed when we prick our hand on a sharp pin. These are, in fact, two quite separate tasks and it is only in a school essay that we are likely to find them linked together. The artificiality of such tasks in itself creates problems for writers in the organization of their texts. In this particular instance the writer has coped remarkably well. However, this text was the only wholly successful one out of a class of over twenty.

As well as managing the organization of the text as a whole successfully, the writer uses a range of cohesive devices to link sentences together. In the commentary on the 'Smoking' drafts we noticed how sentences there tended to be linked by lexical chains. In this text, although there are clearly defined lexical chains, there are many other means used to provide cohesion. For instance, in S3 *This* is used to refer back to S2 as a whole. Such usage allows the writer to break up the proposition that spans sentences 2 and 3 in a way that is helpful to the reader. S5 is a pivot in the organization of the first section of the text. *This latter fact* refers back to S4 while *the two categories* refers forward to S6. In the second part of the text the organizational problems are simpler, but, nonetheless, the writer displays good control over the devices used. *This pain* in S9 links back to S8; *It* in S10 links back to S9; *Here* links sentences 10 and 11; *The same chemical* refers back to S11.

In addition we find time adverbials used to mark the stages of the process *then . . . then . . . finally*. This use of time adverbials illustrates clearly the point about chronological and non-chronological writing made in chapter 2. The first part of the text has no chronology and, therefore, cannot be organized in a time-related manner. The second part is, in effect, a short narrative but it is a typical narrative in the sense that it describes a process that is always occurring – not a once and for all sequence of events; therefore it is properly in the present tense.

Detailed studies of cohesion in texts can be found in Halliday and Hasan 1976, Quirk *et al.* 1985 and Harris and Wilkinson 1986.

CONCLUSION

These 'readings' of texts written under a variety of classroom conditions by both L1 and L2 writers serve to emphasize the complexity of responding to and assessing writing. Responses may be needed in the process of creating the text through the stages of drafting and revising and also to the final product, the finished text. Adequate responses will need to draw upon a range of understandings and these understandings are the ones that have been addressed in this book:

— the purpose and form of writing;
— the audience for writing;
— its organization;
— the processes of creating a text;
— the stage of development of the student;
— the classroom setting, including the support available for the writer;
— the way in which the writing task has been set up;
— and, as has been demonstrated in this final section, assessment needs to engage first and foremost with the communicative purpose and overall coherence and organization of the text, not with localized errors which should be a secondary concern and always related to other primary matters.

Achieving this ideal of understanding is not an easy task. It is, in fact, an ongoing process. With the continual pressure of the school day it may seem unrealistic to expect teachers to read texts written by pupils with the degree of attention that will lead to the sort of adequate response I have been suggesting is necessary. Much will depend on the amount of writing required of pupils and on the way in which the class activities are managed. It is, however, worth reflecting that the quantity of writing produced is of little significance if it does not involve a qualitatively valuable developmental experience for the pupil.

Writing is a complex activity. It is of fundamental importance to learning, to personal development, and to achievement in the education system. As teachers we need to strive continually to find the best ways to help our pupils find fulfilment as writers.

Further reading

Bain, R., B. Fitzgerald and **M. Taylor** (eds.) 1992. *Looking into Language – classroom approaches to knowledge about language.* London: Hodder and Stoughton.

Carter, R. (ed.) 1990. *Knowledge About Language and the Curriculum: the LINC Reader.* London: Hodder and Stoughton.

Christie, F. and **J. Rothery.** 1989. *Writing in Schools* (B.Ed. Course Study Guide). Geelong, Victoria: Deakin University Press.

This student course guide and the accompanying reader provide an ideal introduction to the notion of a genre approach to children's writing.

Halliday, M. A. K. 1989. *Spoken and Written Language.* Oxford: Oxford University Press.

This is a full and very readable guide to the subject. It is indispensible reading for anyone seriously interested in children and language.

Harris, J. and **J. Wilkinson.** 1986. *Reading Children's Writing – a linguistic view.* London: Allen and Unwin.

This is one of the very few attempts to relate recent developments in text linguistics to a study of children's writing. The book focuses on classroom implications and contains chapters by a range of contributors. Topics covered include narrative structure, textual organization, vocabulary and grammatical 'errors'.

Hedge, T. 1988. *Writing.* Oxford: Oxford University Press.

Although this is, in effect, a course book for ESL and EFL teaching, it is informed by a deep understanding of the process of writing and the ways this can be related to the classroom.

Krashen, S. 1984. *Writing Research: theory and applications.* Oxford: Pergamon.

This is a succinct study of research into L1 and L2 writing and provides a good introduction.

Kress, G. 1982. *Learning to Write.* London: Routledge.

This is a unique study of children's early writing from a syntactic perspective. It is particularly valuable for the insights offered into the nature of the sentence and its development in early writing.

Kroll, B. (ed.) 1990. *Second Language Writing – research insights for the classroom.* Cambridge: Cambridge University Press.

This is a useful collection of essays, although the main focus is on writing at tertiary level.

LINC (Language in the National Curriculum) Project 1991. Materials for Professional Development.

These useful materials are available from the Department of English Studies, Univerity of Nottingham.

National Writing Project 1989. Walton on Thames: Nelson.

This series of booklets brings together many of the teacher investigations into writing initiated by the NWP in England from 1985 to 1988. The case studies are uneven but, at best, full of exciting innovation. The booklets, like the project, are not strong on theory.

Perera, K. 1984. *Children's Writing and Reading: analysing classroom language.* Oxford: Basil Blackwell.

This is a detailed, informative and meticulous study of children's linguistic development. It is a key book for gaining insights into the acquisition of grammatical competence in the written mode.

Toolan, M. 1988. *Narrative – a critical linguistic introduction.* London: Routledge.

This is a wide-ranging and accessible study of the structures of narrative, including stories by and for children. All the most significant theoretical discussions of narrative from recent years are included and evaluated in a helpful way.

Glossary

affix Affixes, generically, are **morphemes** that can be added to the be--ginning of a word (**prefixes**) or to the end (**suffixes**). Both constititute an important aspect of the English spelling system. Prefixes normally modify the meaning of the root word, expressing, for instance, negation (*un-*, *de-*, and so on). Suffixes commonly change the word class as in *history* → *historical*.

apposition Elements of language (most commonly noun phrases) which have an equal grammatical status are said to be in apposition. For instance, in *I gave Tom, my brother, a camera*, *Tom* and *my brother* have equal status and the appositional phrase *my brother* provides further information about the first noun phrase *Tom*.

assembling strategies see **pre-writing**

chunking This is the process of dividing a text into units for the purpose of analysis. The term is used particularly in situations where the conventional 'chunk' of written language, the sentence, is not an appropriate or useful unit for analysis as in many texts written by young children or in transcriptions of speech.

chronological/non-chronological writing These terms indicate the way in which the subject matter of a text is organized. In a chronologically organized text, the sequence of events that constitutes the subject matter is related to a real or imagined time sequence. Typically, this occurs in a story or in an account of an actual incident. Non-chronological organization takes a variety of forms among which the purposes of classifying, comparing, arguing and hypothesizing are readily identifiable.

clause The clause has the same structure as a simple sentence: that is, it has to have a subject and a verb. It can also have an object, complements and adverbial elements.

Clauses are divided into two main types – main and subordinate (also called dependent). Examples:

Main	Subordinate
She knew	*that it would be difficult*
The car stopped	*when it ran out of petrol*

Sentences that are complex must contain a main clause and one or more subordinate clauses.

coherence   For a text to be fully satisfactory to a reader/listener it is necessary for the concepts, **propositions** or events to be related to each other and to be consistent with the overall subject of the text. This type of unity is referred to as coherence. Coherence refers to the global unity of a text and needs to be distinguished from **cohesion** which is the term used to describe the means by which sentences are linked. It is possible to create a text that has cohesion but no coherence. Such a text will not be satisfactory. coherence, therefore, is the prime requirement for judging the adequacy of a text.

cohesion/cohesive ties   Cohesion refers to the means by which sentences and sometimes larger units of text are linked together grammatically. The particular items that effect linkage between sentences are called cohesive ties. The main types of tie are:

   proforms (notably pronouns) e.g.

Madeleine was listening to some music. She is particularly fond of Mozart.
Here *Madeleine* is replaced by *she* in the second sentence, creating a tie between the two sentences.

   identity signals (particularly the use of *the* and the demonstratives *this*, *that*, *these*, *those*) e.g. *Angela thought she had lost a book. Later, she found the book under a pile of papers.*
As well as the use of *she* to create a tie with *Angela*, the identity of the book that was presumed lost with the book that was found is confirmed by the use of *the book* in the second sentence.

   conjunctions which can usefully be grouped into the following categories:

Additive	e.g.	*Moreover*
Adversative	e.g.	*However*
Causal	e.g.	*Therefore*
Temporal	e.g.	*Then*

It should be noted that cohesion is also created by lexical patterning in a text.

complex sentence   see **sentence**

content word   Also referred to as **lexical words**, content words form the major part of the total vocabulary of a language – including nouns, adjectives and verbs. This group is distinguished from **structure/grammatical words** and is usually characterized as an 'open' set. This means that the group is potentially infinite and can be added to.

co-ordination   This term is used in grammatical analysis to indicate units of equal status that are linked together. Units thus linked can be clauses, phrases or words.

deixis/deictics   Deixis means 'pointing' or 'indicating'. Common deictic words are the demonstratives (*this*, *that*, *these*, *those*), the definite article and the personal pronouns.

embedding   Information within a sentence can be expressed in a compact and concise manner by being contained within another structure. A simple example is: *Rachel had a bowl of her favourite beef noodles.* Here there are two main pieces of information, or **propositions**: *Rachel had a bowl of beef noodles* and *Beef noodles are Rachel's favourite food.* The second proposition is embedded in the first to achieve economy of expression.

expanded noun phrase   This term denotes a noun phrase structure in which additional elements are added to the obligatory element of a noun phrase (the headword). Elements can be added before and/or after the headword. In the following example, *frog* is the headword: *a small green frog sitting on a lily pad*

genre   This term is used in two related ways. A genre, in a broad sense, is a type or species of text in all instances of which certain defining characteristics are to be discerned. Broadly defined genres include, for example, detective stories, epic poems and 'absurdist' plays. The term is now also being used in a more restricted sense to indicate types of texts with common linguistic and structural configurations (such as recounts, reports and narratives).

lexical density   This term refers to the proportion of **lexical/content**

words to **structure words** in a text. In general terms, written texts have a higher lexical density than spoken texts.

lexical word   see **content word**.

loan word   Languages borrow words from each other. French, for instance, has borrowed *le weekend* and *le jazz* from English. English, over the centuries, has borrowed from a wide range of languages, often as a result of colonialization. Many loan words do not conform to native English spelling patterns and help to create the false impression that English spelling is chaotic.

morpheme   Morphemes are the parts of a word that convey meaning. In the analysis of word structure a contrast is made between units that can stand alone and those that cannot. For example, in *walked* there are two morphemes – *walk* which can stand alone and is 'free' and *-ed* which cannot stand alone and is 'bound'. Morphemes need to be distinguished from syllables which carry no meaning and no grammatical status (unless a syllable is identical to a morpheme).

morphophonemic   This is the technical term to describe spelling systems in which both symbol and word form are used to realize the sound structures of the spoken language. For example, *soft* and *soften* do not have an obvious identity in their sounds but the forms of the two words show clearly their family origin.

nominal/nominalization   Nominalization is the process whereby a noun or noun phrase is formed from a word of another class, as in *Its wing beats...* Nominals are words used as nouns, commonly *this* or *that*.

non-chronological   see **chronology/chronological**.

prefix   see **affix**.

pre-writing   This term is widely used to describe the first stage of the process of writing in which a writer will gather ideas, make plans and so on. As is argued in chapter 3, the term can be misleading since many of the activities typical of this first stage of the writing process may well involve some form of writing. For this reason the term **assembling strategies** is preferred.

process writing   In the debates about the teaching of writing this term has

come to indicate a systematic approach usually regarded as consisting of three or four stages:
- Pre-writing
- Drafting
- Revising and editing
- Publishing

Although these stages are often identifiable in the process of writing, there is a danger of process writing being seen as an inflexible system which emphasizes the operational aspects of the process. In fact, the essence of any act of writing is that it is a series of cognitive processes. The operational procedures, such as drafting and revising, should not be allowed to take precedence over the more fundamental need to facilitate the cognitive processes.

proforms These are items which substitute for other items or units. Pronouns are the most commonly occurring set of proforms. *It*, for instance, can substitute for a lexical noun or it can be used to refer to a preceding unit such as a clause or sentence.

proposition This term is used generally to refer to ideas or pieces of information encoded linguistically within a text.

rhetoric Traditionally, the study of rhetoric refers to the skills of public speaking. The popular meaning of the word as indicating bombast and insincerity derives from the ill-favour of the tradition of rhetoric as it declined. The most recent usage is to describe features of literary language such as parallelism and so on.

sentence The only secure way to define a sentence is by its grammatical constituency and usage. Sentences have the same basic structure as the clause – that is:
- Subject
- Verb
- Object
- Complement
- Adjunct/Adverbial

Of these elements only the first two are obligatory in full sentences. Sentences may be:

- simple (consisting of one main clause only)
- co-ordinated (consisting of two or more clauses of equal status)
- complex (consisting of a main clause and one or more subordinated clauses)

situation   Any linguistic act, such as a conversation, takes place in a specific setting and the nature of this setting has a crucial impact on the language used. The effect of situation on language can be readily discerned by listening to a tape recording of a conversation at which one was not present.

structure words   This group of words (also called **grammatical words**) constitutes a finite or 'closed' set. The group comprises items such as conjunctions, prepositions, pronouns, articles and auxiliary and modal verbs. The group is contrasted with **content words**.

subordination   When two clauses or more are linked together in a sentence, they may have equal status and are then termed co-ordinated. If one or more clauses depends on the main clause it is said to be subordinated (or dependent). See also **clause**.

suffix   see **affix**.

References

Britton, J. *et al.* 1975. *The Development of Writing Abilities 11–18.* Basingstoke: Thomas Nelson and Sons Ltd.

Brumfitt, C. 1984. *Communicative Methodology in Language Teaching – the roles of fluency and accuracy.* Cambridge: Cambridge University Press.

Bunton, D. and **C. Green** (eds.) 1991. *English Usage in Hong Kong.* Hong Kong: Institute of Language in Education (ILEJ Special Issue no. 2).

Carter, R. A. 1992. A note on grammar and punctuation. Unpublished manuscript. Dept. of English Studies, University of Nottingham.

Christie, F. 1989. Genres of Writing. In *Writing in Schools* (B.Ed. Course Study Guide). Geelong, Victoria: Deakin University Press.

DES. 1990. *English in the National Curriculum.* London: HMSO.

Eagleton, T. 1983. *Literary Theory.* Oxford: Basil Blackwell.

Emig, J. 1971. The composing processes of 12th graders. NCTE Research Report no. 13. Urbana, Ill.: NCTE.

Halliday, M.A.K. 1989. *Spoken and Written Language.* Oxford: Oxford University Press. (First published 1985 by Deakin University Press.)

Halliday, M. A. K. and **R. Hasan.** 1976. *Cohesion in English.* London: Longman.

Harpin, W. 1976. *The Second 'R'.* London: Allen and Unwin.

Harris, J. 1990. Writing. In J. Harris and J. Wilkinson (eds.) *In the Know – a guide to English language in the National Curriculum.* Cheltenham: Stanley Thornes.

Harris, J. and **J. Wilkinson.** 1986. *Reading Children's Writing – a linguistic view.* London: Allen and Unwin.

Harris, J. and **A. Sanderson.** 1989. *Reasons for Writing – early stages.* Aylesbury: Ginn.

Hoey, M. 1983. *On the Surface of Discourse*. London: Allen and Unwin.

Hoey, M. 1986. Undeveloped discourse: some factors affecting the adequacy of children's non-fictional written discourses. In J. Harris and J. Wilkinson. *Reading Children's Writing – a linguistic view*. London: Allen and Unwin.

Hunt, K. 1965. Grammatical structures written at three grade levels. Research Report no. 3 Urbana, Ill.: NCTE.

Krashen, S. 1984. *Writing Research:* theory and applications. Oxford: Pergamon.

Kress, G. 1982. *Learning to Write*. London: Routledge & Keegan Paul.

Kroll, B. (ed.) 1990. *Second Language Writing – research insights for the classroom*. Cambridge: Cambridge University Press.

Labov, W. 1972. *Language in the Inner City*. Oxford: Basil Blackwell.

La Brant, L. 1933. A study of certain language developments in children. *Genetic Psychology Monographs*, 14.

Loban, W. 1963. The language of elementary school children. Research Report no. 1. Urbana, Ill.: NCTE.

Loban, W. 1976. Language development: kindergarden through grade twelve. Research Report no. 18. Urbana, Ill.: NCTE.

Longacre, R. 1976. *An Anatomy of Speech Notions*. Lisse: Peter de Ridder.

McKay, S. (ed.) 1984. *Composing in a Second Language*. Rowley, Mass.: Newbury House.

Martin, J. and J. Rothery. 1980. *Writing Project Paper 1*. Sydney: Dept. of Linguistics, University of Sydney.

Moffett, J. 1968. *Teaching the Universe of Discourse*. Boston: Houghton Mifflin.

O'Rourke, P. 1990. Spoken and written language. In J. Harris and J. Wilkinson (eds.) *In the Know – a guide to English language in the National Curriculum*. Cheltenham: Stanley Thornes.

Perera, K. 1984. *Children's Writing and Reading: analysing classroom language*. Oxford: Basil Blackwell.

Pianko, S. 1979. A description of the composing process of college freshmen writers. *Research in the Teaching of English*, 13, 5–22.

Quirk, R. *et al.* 1985. *A Comprehensive Grammar of the English Language*. London: Longman.

Savva, H. 1990. The multilingual classroom. In J. Harris and J. Wilkinson

References

(eds.) *In the Know – a guide to English language in the National Curriculum.* Cheltenham: Stanley Thornes.

Stallard, K. 1988. *Encouraging Confidence in Writers.* Sheffield: Language Development Centre, Sheffield-Hallam University.

Swales, J. 1990. *Genre Analysis.* Cambridge: Cambridge University Press.

Toolan, M. 1988. *Narrative – a critical linguistic introduction.* London: Routledge.

Wales, L. 1990. Literacy for learners of English as a second language. In F. Christie (ed.) *Literacy for a Changing World.* Victoria: ACER.

Winter, E. 1977. A clause-relational approach to English texts – a study of some predictive lexical items in written discourse. *Instructional Science*, 6, 1, 1–92.

Index

Note To avoid too many entries occurring as subheadings of 'writing' I have preferred to list under the feature of writing – thus 'writing development' is listed under 'development of writing'.